ABORTION
The Agonizing Decision

Suddenly, she banged her fist on the table. "Look, *there's never going to be anything easy about an abortion. It isn't easy. No girl will ever make the decision simply. No matter what anyone says, it can't ever be just five unpleasant minutes. The law, the church, stupid morals have nothing to do with the way a woman feels when she makes a decision like this. She herself knows how painful, difficult, complicated it all is. . . ."*

Romy Schneider, West German actress,
quoted in *Life*

ABORTION
The Agonizing Decision

DAVID R. MACE

Nashville • ABINGDON PRESS • *New York*

ABORTION: THE AGONIZING DECISION
Copyright © 1972 by Abingdon Press

ISBN 0-687-00654-6 (paper)

ISBN 0-687-00653-8 (cloth)

Library of Congress Catalog Card Number: 70-187590

MANUFACTURED BY THE PARTHENON PRESS AT
NASHVILLE, TENNESSEE, UNITED STATES OF AMERICA

Preface

I have written this book primarily because I am concerned about the predicament of the woman with a "problem pregnancy," who is presented today with the opportunity to have an abortion legally, but is deeply perplexed as to whether this is what she really wants. I find that she often lacks information about what abortion really is; what it might do to her physically and emotionally; whether it is right or wrong, and why.

Often she doesn't know where to get accurate, unbiased information. Discussion with relatives and friends often turns out to be a process of "pooling ignorance." Yet she hesitates to go immediately to a physician or other professional person, because that might imply that she definitely wants an abortion; whereas her real need is to make a wise decision as to whether she does or she doesn't.

When she turns to written material, she finds that the controversy has been focused upon whether or not society should sanction legal abortion; not upon how the woman, given this right, can exercise it in accordance with her individual value system. Few writers stress that abortion can be either right or wrong, depending on the woman concerned and on the particular circumstances; that it is a subject of such great complexity that generalizations offer little help. What the woman wants is information rather than opinions; above all else she needs a counselor who will not impose his views, but enable her freely to make up her own mind.

After ranging widely through the literature on the subject, and discussing it with medical colleagues, with pastors, with lawyers, with teachers, and, not least, with women young and old, I came to the conclusion that I should myself try to write the kind of book I seemed unable to find.

Although the book is written first and foremost for the pregnant woman who needs counseling help, I hope it may also be useful, both as a guide and as a tool, to professional people who are approached by women considering abortion. I particularly hope that it may encourage the provision of better abortion counseling services.

Finally, I believe the book should be of interest to the general reader who wants to weigh the controversial facts about abortion interpreted from many viewpoints.

I wish to thank three of my colleagues on the faculty of Wake Forest University—John P. Gusdon, Jr., M.D., Associate Professor of Obstetrics and Gynecology; McLeod G. Bryan, Ph.D., Professor of Religion; Pasco M. Bowman, Ph.D., Dean, School of Law. They kindly read the sections of the book which lie in their respective fields, and made many helpful suggestions. I acknowledge also my increasing debt of gratitude to my devoted secretary, Mrs. Lucy Crawford, who with the help of Mrs. Jane Mall, transformed my untidy scribblings into pages of clear and orderly typescript.

DAVID R. MACE

Contents

Prologue:
The Woman in Crisis

"I am pregnant." From time immemorial, this awareness has brought to women their greatest joys and their highest hopes. Down the long corridors of the centuries and across the vast spaces of the millenia; back through the million years, perhaps two million years, of man's struggle to survive and to create a viable society, this has been the most exciting news a woman could share with the significant other people in her life.

"I am pregnant." She has said it with pride, with the deep, satisfying knowledge that now she had found her real identity. Now she was truly a woman, now she would win the acceptance and the respect that were her due. In the awareness of the mystery and the drama unfolding deep within her, she was able to draw herself up to her full stature, to hold up her head proudly, to look the whole world unflinchingly in the face.

"I am pregnant." Yes, but you are not happy, not proud. The awareness of your condition stirs in you not delight and hope, but misery and despair. What has happened deep within your body is for you not a triumph, but a tragedy. As you face the world, you are filled with dismay. When you are confronted by the significant people in your life, your response is to avert your head, to lower your eyes. Pregnancy for you is not joy, but sorrow; not pride, but shame; not satisfaction, but disillusionment.

Perhaps you are young and unmarried. Pregnancy was not part of your plans. You took chances, and you knew it. But you hoped it wouldn't happen. Maybe you took steps to avoid it, but something went wrong. What do you do now? It just wouldn't make sense to get married. Your boyfriend doesn't mean as much as that to you—or you don't mean as much as that to him. Or, maybe you *do* hope to marry him someday, but not now—you must complete your education first; you just aren't ready to establish a home and set up a family yet. Even to have a baby and offer it for adoption would complicate life so much for you that you don't see how you could do it. This pregnancy is just a misfortune. It has come at the wrong time and thrown your whole life into confusion.

Perhaps you are married. You certainly do plan to have children—but not yet. You and your husband are in a situation right now that makes a pregnancy very unwelcome. You have no home and very little money, or you are about to make a major move, or you have a job that you can't give up, or you have been seriously ill and you can't face a major new responsibility; maybe it's your husband who is very much against having a baby now. It is even possible that the child would not be his. . . . This pregnancy could threaten your health, your career, your marriage.

Perhaps you already have as many children as you feel able to raise, and another child would make demands that you just couldn't meet. You haven't the resources—space, money, energy—to cope with a young baby and do justice as well to the legitimate needs of your husband and your other children. This pregnancy is unwelcome. It was an accident. It was no part of your plans to have another child. You just feel overwhelmed at the prospect.

Perhaps you are a middle-aged wife whose children are all in their teens. You feel you have done your duty as a mother and raised your family. You and your husband have been looking forward to a period of greater leisure, to a quiet life together after the strenuous task of being parents. The prospect of starting all over again overwhelms you. It would shatter all your plans. You just don't see how you could possibly face it.

Perhaps tragedy has invaded your life. You have been deceived by an unscrupulous man, exploited and now abandoned, and a new life is beginning within you that you resent and cannot accept. Or, your doctor has told you that the child you very much want may turn out to be handicapped or deformed. The prospect of motherhood under these conditions is a hideous nightmare.

Perhaps, perhaps, perhaps. There are many variations of the theme—the possibilities are endless. Each woman's personal story is unique. Your pregnancy may hold for you nothing but horror. It may simply be unwelcome or embarrassing or inconvenient. You may be genuinely confused about whether to be glad or sorry, whether to accept it or to wish it would go away.

THE NEED FOR DECISION

One thing is clear: You must do something, or rather, you must decide what to do. Pregnancies do sometimes

end of their own accord—but you can't count on that.
You need a policy, a plan, and you need it without delay.
Every day that passes, the developing life within you grows
bigger, more active, more mature. Nine months seems a
long time, but it can pass very quickly.

The decision that confronts you is quite clear. Unless
the matter is taken out of your hands and you have a miscarriage, you have only two choices—to allow the pregnancy to go through or to terminate it.

For some women, there is no choice to be made. There
are those who simply believe that abortion is wrong and
wouldn't consider it. Whatever solution they find for their
problem, the pregnancy cannot be interrupted. There are
also women for whom choice presents no problem. If they
find themselves with pregnancies they don't want, the solution is obvious—just get rid of it, and that's that.

The probability is that women who hold either of those
views will not be reading this book. It would be my guess,
also, that women who have such final and clear-cut attitudes constitute a very small minority in our culture today.
The vast majority, I believe, are confused and unable to
make up their minds about what they would do if they
were confronted personally with the problem. Even if they
think they have taken up a position, there are still lingering
doubts and uncertainties in their minds. In most instances,
they feel they don't know enough about what is involved
to arrive at a clear decision. The subject is a very complicated one. Someday, they keep promising themselves,
they will go into it more thoroughly and get the facts
straight.

I am going to assume that you are in this category. But
now the matter can't be put off any longer. You are preg-

nant, and you must make up your mind. You have a personal decision to make, and it is urgent.

I have written this book with the express purpose of offering you help. I believe the decision whether to have or not to have an abortion is one of the most agonizing choices with which, as a woman, you can be confronted. It touches you at a very profound level, because it has to do with the one function that makes womanhood really distinctive—motherhood. It involves deep and complex emotions. It represents a very private and personal matter, which it may not be easy to talk over with the people closest to you. Even if you *can* talk with them, they are so much involved that they will almost certainly try to influence you to accept their way of thinking, when your desperate need is to be allowed to come to your own personal decision. If you talk to friends and associates, they are not likely to be well informed on the subject and will probably serve up some opinion they have taken secondhand from an advocate of some particular point of view. There are deep differences of opinion in our culture at the present time.

So, what do you do? I believe your greatest need is for counseling; and it is my hope that we shall soon be able to provide this for women in your present predicament. If you can find a wise counselor—one who knows the subject really well, but is also a patient listener; one who will encourage and help you to think this issue through, to come to terms with your conflicting emotions, and to arrive at a decision you can live with—if you can find such a counselor, beat a path to his or her door and count yourself fortunate. For this decision can have far-reaching consequences for your future life, and arriving at it will involve a very profound encounter with yourself and hopefully a clarification of your needs in life, your values, and your goals.

This book cannot provide a substitute for a good counselor, yet it is being written in the hope that it can offer *some* help to the woman who doesn't know where to turn. The counseling must of necessity be one-sided, and that's a serious limitation. But in the absence of anything better, I hope I can help you. Let me explain how we shall go about it.

WHAT WE PLAN TO DO

In trying to help you, I have two aims. I want to provide you with some *knowledge* about abortion—the facts as far as we know them today. I want also to give you some *personal help* about how to face this issue and make the best choice you possibly can.

Let's take the knowledge first. Obviously, you want direct, specific information about abortion as a medical operation and what it will mean to you. But I think you also need knowledge of a wider kind—knowledge of how other people think and feel, and have thought and felt, about abortion. There are moral issues as well as practical issues, and no responsible woman would want to ignore them. The decision you have to make must do more than solve your immediate problem. It must also be a decision, as far as possible, that you can live with for the rest of your life.

Is all this knowledge really necessary? Yes, I think so. To be sure, you could make a decision without knowing the facts. But you can make a better decision if you have them in your mind. It is true that personal choices come out of your inner feelings as you straighten them out and reconcile them with each other. But your feelings are very much af-

16

fected by your understanding, or misunderstanding, of the implications of the decision you have to make. History is full of stories of people who made poor decisions because they were poorly informed. The shipwrecked sailor is much better able to decide which direction to take if he has a map in his hands.

In the case of abortion, we are dealing with something about which we have had very little accurate knowledge in the past. It has in fact been a subject we didn't normally discuss at all. So we have no tradition that has been handed down, no models on which to base our own behavior, no clear signals to show us the right way. You have to do your own thinking for yourself; and for this it is essential that you have sound and accurate knowledge of the facts. You may not need all of them, and you can discard what doesn't seem to affect your personal decision; but all the basic facts should be available to you.

Your other need is to sort out your own tangled thoughts and feelings and make a good decision. This is where counseling can really help you. Most people find that they can see themselves more clearly when they are able to talk, freely and without restraint, about themselves. It gives you a welcome sense of support to know that someone else knows everything about you—someone who will not judge or condemn, will not try to take over and manage your life, but will accept you as you are and help you to draw upon your own inner resources to meet the crisis that confronts you.

It helps too when the counselor knows about the problem you face, has seen others go through it, so that he can help you to look squarely at all the alternatives open to you and to consider their possibilities and their limitations. He should be able to guide you through the complicated process of decision-making, not trying to influence your choice, but leaving you entirely free to use your own judgment and to arrive at your own conclusion.

As far as it is possible outside a real-life situation where two people actually confront each other, my aim will be to try to provide this kind of counseling help.

INTRODUCING THE COUNSELOR

Since I am to be your counselor, I should now introduce myself. Let me start with the fact that I am a man, and let me say that I frankly consider this to be a disadvantage. The abortion decision lies in an area of human life of which a man can have no personal experience. Besides, a woman considering an abortion may not, at that particular time in her life, be kindly disposed toward men in general, because she is painfully aware of the fact that one of them got her into the awkward situation where she now is. So I am of the opinion that women counselors are ideal. I therefore accept my limitations and will do my best to overcome them.

I am now in my sixties and a professor in a medical school, where my task as a behavioral scientist has been to help my medical colleagues and students to understand and deal with the human aspects of their patients' lives. I owe a great deal to the women in my life. I have one sister, one wife, two daughters, and three granddaughters. I love them all dearly and value my relationships with them. Professionally, I have devoted most of my life to developing marriage-counseling services and education for family life in many countries in the world. During more than thirty years I have counseled with so many young people and so many husbands and wives, that I have no idea now of their total number. I have listened to their personal stories about their sexual and marital problems and done my best to help them. I have of course also counseled with many women who found themselves unexpectedly pregnant and had to make the agonizing decision that now confronts you.

What is my personal position about abortion? A good counselor should be able to help people whatever his personal views and values happen to be, because his focus should be on helping them to reach whatever decision is comfortable and acceptable to them. No doubt some of my personal views will emerge in this book, although I shall try to take a neutral position, which I think will serve my purpose best.

SETTING THE STAGE

I have considered carefully how I can best provide you with the help you need—background knowledge and personal guidance in making your decision. Here is what I have decided.

I will tell you the story of my counseling with one woman who had to make the agonizing decision. I will take her with me to an abortion conference where well-qualified speakers will tell us, simply and clearly, what we ought to know about abortion. I will discuss with her afterwards what the speakers have said and how she has reacted to what she has learned. I will also discuss with her how she feels about her predicament and how she can come to terms with her emotions. And I will try to give her guidelines to help her in her difficult task of decision-making. You will share all these experiences with us and identify with her as far as you can. I hope you will also carry out the simple assignments I shall give her.

She must have a name, so I will call her Helen. Why? I don't know. It happened to be the first name that came into my head. Maybe I was thinking of Helen of Troy, who was very beautiful, very attractive to men, but nevertheless found herself in a great deal of trouble.

Is Helen a real person? Yes and no. She represents a great many women who have come to me for counseling. So she is not one woman, but many women in one. And she has to be a very remarkable woman, because she must represent a great many other women too. You and you and you who are my readers. It was said of Helen of Troy that her face launched a thousand ships, and it will have to be equally true of this Helen that her voice represents the voices of a thousand women. That is no easy task.

So now let me introduce Helen. She has been referred to me by her pastor. She sought a private interview with him, told him about her pregnancy and that she was considering an abortion but couldn't make up her mind. He discussed this with her but decided that since her situation was a very complicated one, she should have further help. He asked me if I could see her within a few days, and I agreed to do so. This was a Monday evening.

One thing about abortion counseling is that there is no time to waste. So I called up Helen at once, made sure she was alone and could talk freely on the phone, and made plans with her. We arranged an appointment for Thursday evening at my home. Then I asked her to keep all day Saturday free—this was the occasion of the Abortion Conference, and I wanted her to come to it with me. She was interested and readily agreed to do this.

I'm not going to tell you any more about Helen. I won't even tell you her personal story. I have arrived at this decision because I think it will be easier for you to identify

with her if you don't know the facts about her age, education, religion, marital status, and so on. Giving you these
details would only stress the *differences* between you and
her. I want to stress the *similarities* shared by all women
faced with your present dilemma.

I had a further telephone talk with Helen. After my first
Monday evening call to her, I gave a good deal of thought
to what we should do and called her again later to give her
an assignment. I asked her to spend an hour or so writing
out, in the form of a letter to me, her personal account of
how she came to be pregnant and why she was thinking of
seeking an abortion. I told her not to bother at all about
writing style, spelling, or anything like that—just put down
on paper how she saw her problem, with the facts about
herself, her background, and the significant other people
in her life, including, of course, the man by whom she was
pregnant. When she asked me whether there was any
special way in which I wanted this set out, I said no; I
wanted her to do it in whatever way came naturally to her.
I asked her to mail this letter to me or to bring it when she
came for her Thursday appointment.

I would like to ask you, if you are willing, to undertake
this same assignment. You may ask, what's the sense of
writing a letter when you don't have an appointment with
a counselor and don't even have a counselor? My answer is
that I think you will find it a helpful experience anyway.
All of us, when we are anxious and depressed, tend to get
into a very emotional state in which we can easily get confused about our facts. One of the values of counseling is
what we call catharsis, the process of speaking out your
troubles—what we call "getting it off your chest." This
usually brings a feeling of relief, and it also usually enables
you to see your situation in clearer perspective. Of course,

in a counseling situation someone else is listening, and that helps a lot. But what many people don't know is that even if no one is listening, the experience is still a helpful one.

I invite you to put this to the test. If writing is troublesome to you, there's another way you can do it. Find a place where you can be sure of being alone and secure against interruption—if at all possible, a place where you can talk out loud without danger of being overheard. Then tell your whole story to an imaginary counselor, letting all your feelings flow out freely. I know most of us feel a bit awkward about doing anything like this because there's a widespread idea that people who talk to themselves are crazy. Don't believe it. Talking to yourself is a very sensible and helpful procedure. The proper name for it is soliloquy, and you will find it often in plays—specially in Shakespeare's plays. Many people do it in real life, too, and find it most helpful.

That, then, is your first assignment. I invite you to undertake it—either by writing or by speaking aloud. I shall have two more assignments for Helen—and you—later.

First Conversation
with Helen

It is Thursday evening, at eight o'clock. Helen has come, as arranged, to my home where I often see people for evening appointments and where there is more privacy than in my office at the medical school.

"Helen, we don't really know each other yet. We've just talked on the phone. All I know now is that you're pregnant, and you're thinking of having an abortion, but you can't make up your mind about it. That's a state of affairs that could make anyone nervous and anxious. Is that the way you're feeling right now?"

"Yes, that's about it, I guess."

"Have you ever sought counseling before—of any kind?"

"Not really. I've asked friends for advice and been to my doctor, and I once had an interview with a guidance counselor when I was at school. But nothing like this."

"Well, now you've made the trip and you're here, how do you feel about coming? Apprehensive?"

"Yes, a bit. But I'm glad I'm here, too. I've been very

worried about this decision. It was hard to make up my mind when my pastor suggested an appointment with you. But now I'm sure I did the right thing, so I have a sense of relief."

"Helen, just how do you see my role in this counseling? How do you imagine I can best help you?"

"Well, for a start, I know you can't make the decision for me. And I don't want you to. A few of my friends who know about my problem have been trying to do that already, and they've got me more confused than I was before. This has got to be my own decision and no one else's.

"What I need is to see this thing straight. I really don't know anything about abortion. I just never thought of myself as a candidate for it. So it was something out on the edge of my life—a general fact that I had never had to consider personally, so I didn't really need to know about it. Now that's all changed, and I find myself suddenly faced with something I don't understand at all."

"Let me start by saying that I got your letter, and I've read it through twice. It gave me a very clear picture of your predicament. So I feel I know quite a lot about you already. Would you care to tell me, quite candidly, how you felt about writing it?"

"It seemed a little odd at first, I must say, that I should write you a letter when I had just made an appointment to see you. But you were obviously quite sincere about wanting me to do it. So I sat down right away, after your second phone call, and started to write. I got completely absorbed in it, and wrote on till my arm ached. You suggested I should spend an hour on it. Actually I went on for more than two hours. It cleared my mind in a way that quite surprised me."

"Good. So let me explain what we're going to do now.

24

We are going to talk about a woman's emotions as she finds herself with an unwelcome pregnancy. I'm going to ask you about this, and you're going to report quite naturally how you feel."

"I'm ready."

"All right. Helen, I'd like you to talk about the emotions that swept over you at various times, from the point at which you became aware that you were pregnant and wished you weren't?"

"I'd say I've been through a whole tumult of emotions—anxiety, fear, panic, anger, guilt, exasperation, frustration, despair. But I know you don't want a list—you want a kind of description of what I've been feeling. Well, of course, it all started up on the day my period was due and nothing happened. By itself, that wasn't a big issue—I knew it could easily be late. But when you know you *could* be pregnant, and you don't want to be, of course, you begin to wonder. It's like a small dark cloud in an otherwise bright sky—you don't take it very seriously, yet you know it *could* bring a storm.

"Well, the next day came, and the next, and still no period. By this time I was having waves of apprehension. I did the usual routine things, and when I was busy and talking to people I was my normal self. But every now and then, when nothing much was happening, an ice-cold hand seemed to grip me, and a sort of shudder went through me. Then I'd pull myself together and tell myself there was no need to worry yet—my period could start at any time.

"When it was later than I'd ever had to wait for a period before, I was plain scared to death. It was as if a little voice kept saying over and over again, deep down inside me—'You're pregnant.' It was a cruel, mocking, accusing voice, and every time it spoke it seemed like a hammerblow striking a raw nerve. I was in a pretty desperate state. While I was with other people, I had to hide my feelings, though I don't know how I did it. But when I was alone, I seemed to be standing on the edge of an abyss. I prayed. I cried. I clenched my fists and stamped my feet in anger. When I was in the bathroom I looked at myself in the mirror, as though I expected to see some terrible change in my face. It was wonderful to fall asleep at night, but I kept waking again. Just for a minute I would feel like my old self; then the awareness of my pregnancy swept over me like a cold, dark wave, and I sank into the depths of despair.

"I seemed to be completely obsessed by feelings of dread. I lost my appetite. I couldn't get interested in the things I usually enjoyed. I had to put on a big act to cover up my feelings, and I often made excuses to get away from people because the effort of trying to behave normally made me feel completely exhausted."

She pauses, and looks at me inquiringly.

"Helen, I think you have described your anguish very vividly. I wonder if you could now analyze some of your specific feelings. The big one, that came early on, seems to have been fear in various forms—anxiety, apprehension, panic. In general—leave out your personal specifics—what were you afraid of?"

"Well, I guess I felt trapped. I saw nothing but trouble ahead, and I just couldn't face it. But that isn't answering your question. What was I afraid of? It isn't easy to generalize it, though I know that's what you want. I suppose I faced disaster, and the awareness paralyzed me. I felt I just couldn't cope with what was coming to me."

"I believe one of the major fears of women in your situation is the fear of rejection. That's true specially of the unmarried girl who sees her pregnancy as a disgrace and imagines that all the nice, kind people in her world will recoil from her in horror, as though she were a leper. A married woman pregnant by another man might likewise fear rejection by her husband and the breakup of her home. Another major fear which a married woman might have would be the feeling that a child coming at this time would shatter all her plans and put her in a situation with which she just couldn't cope. These are forms of fear I have often found in women with whom I have counseled. But let's turn to another strong emotion—anger. You talked of exasperation and frustration. What were you angry about?"

"I've considered that. Basically I think I had a strong feeling of suffering injustice. Why do we women have to be put in this kind of situation? It isn't fair. Partly I suppose it's because the woman always suffers, whereas the man gets by more easily. And then it's anger toward other people in general, for being so lacking in understanding of a woman's predicament. I have confided in a few people I feel I can trust, and they have tried to help. But they just don't really seem to understand what I'm going through, and the advice they offer sometimes seems so silly and so inadequate.

"I feel angry, too, because everything seems so topsy-turvy. Getting pregnant should be a wonderful experience —that's what being a woman is mostly about. I see mothers with their children, and I tell myself that they were once where I am now, and probably they were thrilled and happy about it. And yet here am I, utterly miserable. Why does it have to be that way? This is certainly part of my anger— because something good has gone sour for me."

"You left out anger against men, perhaps to spare my feelings. But that must really boil up in the girl abused or exploited by an irresponsible male who took advantage of her or led her on with false promises or assurances of love.

And something like that must also be true of the married woman whose husband made her pregnant against her will, by exploitation or carelessness. Even when the man isn't directly to blame, she could be angry with him because he doesn't show real compassion or understanding—like the husband who tells her in an offhand way to 'get rid of it,' as though that were a thing that could be easily done.

"You spoke of anger against society. And you are so right. We have handled these delicate human situations so badly. We won't face up to giving our children sex education, then we judge them harshly when ignorance lands them in trouble. We turn a blind eye to all kinds of sexual games that have always gone on beneath the surface and even makes jokes about them; but when a woman gets trapped in a pregnancy and found out, we suddenly become very moral and condemn her.

"I can see that anger is one of the strong emotions you have to cope with. What about anger against yourself? You did mention guilt, I think?"

"Yes, I did. And I *have* had to live with that. As the whole thing goes round and round in my mind, and I try to figure out who's to blame, I have to come back to myself and say 'If only. . . .' And I could give you a long list of things I've figured out—things I might have done differently so that this wouldn't have happened to me. But what's the use of all the figuring? I come back in the end to the hard truth. It *has* happened, and I can't wish it away."

"And is that the point at which despair takes over?"

"Yes. The big black cloud covers the whole sky. The lights go out, and you're left shivering in the dark. It's an awful feeling. There seems no way out. So you think of suicide. I've been through that too. You get to the point where you're so numb with despair, so sick with the whole thing, so utterly tired of struggling with it and screwing your face into a smile when your heart is breaking, that you say to yourself 'Wouldn't it be easier just to end it all?' I've thought that, Dr. Mace. Is that awfully bad of me? Do other women go through this too?"

"Yes, Helen, a great many of them, in my experience, go through just what you've been describing. And when a woman gets as low as that, the idea of abortion must look like a glimmer of light in a dark tunnel. Tell me how you see this, Helen."

"It's just as you say. It's the one bit of light you can see anywhere. Don't get me wrong—as a woman I shrink from the whole idea—I'm sure every woman does. But when you're in a state of mind in which you have seriously considered doing away with yourself, and you know there's a way of solving your problem—something you can do fairly easily and quickly, without anyone having to know about it—it gives you hope. It means you really *can* wish it away. It's really possible for you to go back to the point where you felt like a normal human being and could hold up your head in the presence of other people. That's what abortion offers—a way out of a desperate situation, an answer to despair."

"Helen, I fully understand your predicament. Abortion *is* a very attractive proposition for a woman in your situation. If that is your considered judgment, I will accept it and support you in acting on it. But I want you first to look at all these feelings—very mixed feelings—that surge through you and be sure you understand them. This can be your second assignment. If you like, write them down as questions: Why am I afraid? Why am I angry? Why do I feel guilty? Then answer them to the best of your ability, being as honest with yourself as you know how to be.

"Let me explain clearly why I'm setting you this second assignment. Faced with the kind of critical decision you're going to make in the next few days, I want to be sure that you are in touch with your deepest feelings and that you understand what they are telling you about yourself. Whatever your final decision turns out to be, I don't want you to be assailed afterward by doubts about it. Unless you have really faced your feelings at the time, you could easily be tortured afterward with the thought that you acted in a state of unbalanced emotion and that you made a mistake. I don't want this to happen to you."

"I understand. Our talk tonight has been very helpful to me—just being able to express my feelings, and to have them accepted. I feel more relaxed than I have for what seems like a very long time."

"All right, Helen, I think we've talked as much now as is good for us. Let me get your coat. I'll see you again on Saturday morning at nine o'clock, at the Lincoln Hotel. Bring a notebook."

ONE-DAY CONFERENCE ON ABORTION

*Organized by the County Federation
of Women's Clubs and Organizations*

PROGRAM

8:30- 9:00 A.M.	Registration
9:00- 9:50 A.M.	"The World Within The Womb"— Dr. William Archer
10:00-10:50 A.M.	"Attitudes to Abortion, Past and Present"—Dr. Arthur Ferguson
11:00-11:50 A.M.	"The Liberalizing of Abortion: A World Perspective"—Dr. Lawrence Kolb
12:00- 1:50 P.M.	Lunch and Recess
2:00- 2:50 P.M.	"The Value of Unborn Life: A Dialogue"—Monsignor Kenneth Overton and Dr. Alice Thompson
3:00- 3:50 P.M.	"The Need for Abortion Counseling" —Dr. David R. Mace and Reactor Panel
4:00 P.M.	Adjournment

The Abortion Conference, Session 1— "The World Within the Womb"

It is 9:00 A.M. on Saturday in the Peacock Room at the Lincoln Hotel. About a hundred women are in the audience —representatives of women's organizations in the county. On the platform is Mrs. Cynthia Boyd, President of the Wednesday Morning Club, who is to be chairman of the conference. With her is Dr. William Archer, the first speaker.

"Good morning, ladies. Welcome to our conference. I'm Cynthia Boyd, and I'm to be your chairman today. I think you all know why we're here. Now that the new abortion law has been passed, we feel we should know more about this very controversial subject. In our organizations we have been discussing what we ought to do to provide confidential counseling for women in our community who are asking for it. After today's conference, some of you may decide to offer your services for abortion counseling. If enough of you do so, we'll follow this up with a training course. But today our purpose is to get an overall picture of a complicated subject which most of us don't know much about.

"We have some distinguished speakers with us today. The first is here at my side. It is my pleasure to introduce to you Dr. William Archer, who is a professor in the Department of Obstetrics and Gynecology here at our medical school. Many of you already know him. In fact, some of you know him very well, because he helped to bring your babies into the world!

"We have asked Dr. Archer to start our conference by telling us the basic things we ought to know about abortion from the medical point of view. Dr. Archer, we are delighted to have you with us today."

"Thank you, Mrs. Boyd. You must all be aware that for a physician abortion presents a difficult problem. The practice of medicine is devoted to the saving and preserving of human life, and we doctors are dedicated to that goal. To perform abortions is not easy for us, and some physicians are unwilling to do it at all. But we have to face realities today. We know that where abortion is not available legally to women, many of them get it illegally. The business of illegal abortion—'backstreet surgery,' as we call it—has been one of the most disreputable features of our civilized life. It has taken the lives, unnecessarily, of some women and done permanent damage to the health of others. Our hope is that now, by making abortion possible under safe, sanitary, hospital conditions, we can greatly reduce all that. We are therefore willing, though always with some natural reluctance, to put our medical skill at the disposal of women for whom an abortion seems the best solution to an acute and distressing personal situation, insofar as the law permits us to do so.

"So let me turn to the subject of my talk. I have given it the title 'The World Within the Womb.'

"Mrs. Boyd has asked me to assume that your knowledge is limited and to go over the facts with you carefully. I shall do so in the simplest possible terms, avoiding complications and technicalities as far as I can. This will mean that I shall have to oversimplify my account, and at some points it will mean some sacrifice of strict scientific accuracy. But this won't matter because what you need to know are just the general facts.

"When a woman conceives a child, that is the beginning of the process of reproduction. It happens as a result of having sexual intercourse with a man. When he reaches his climax, the seminal fluid passes out of the end of the penis and forms a pool somewhere near the entrance to her uterus (the womb). This fluid normally contains hundreds of millions of *sperms* (the full name is the Greek plural spermatozoa), which are like tiny tadpoles, far too small to be seen by the human eye, except through a microscope. The sperms swim by lashing their long tails back and forth, and unless they are prevented, many of them get into the womb and on beyond into the tubes, in one of which an egg cell (or *ovum*, which is just the Latin word for 'egg') may be waiting. When a sperm meets an ovum, and both are healthy, they join together into one new cell. It requires just one sperm, out of all the millions that started the race, to join with an ovum. When this happens, we say the ovum has been fertilized; and that is what it means for a woman to conceive. Once she has a fertilized ovum in one of her tubes, she can become pregnant and have a baby, normally about nine months later.

"The process of growing begins at once when sperm and ovum have joined together. The new cell is called a *zygote*, from a Greek word that means 'joined'. It has a power that neither sperm nor ovum had alone—the power to split into

34

two cells, each of which in turn has the power to split into two more. This process of dividing and dividing goes on and on—that is how the baby develops. First there is one cell, then two, then four, then eight, then sixteen—on and on the process goes, until the cells run into millions and eventually billions.

"A cell is the simplest form of life—although it is in fact far from simple. In order to divide into two new cells it must grow to double its size. And in order to double its size it must have food. The ovum which the woman releases each month carries a large supply of cell food. That is why it is much, much bigger than the sperm released by the man. The ovum is in fact, compared with the sperm, a huge mass of cell food. But somewhere inside it there is a tiny cell, called the *nucleus,* which is exactly the same size as the head of the sperm and made up in exactly the same way. It isn't quite correct to say that the sperm unites with the ovum. It unites with the nucleus of the ovum, and in doing so, it drops off its tail, which it no longer needs.

"A very simple way of picturing this is to think of the ovum as a boat loaded with food, floating down a canal. The boat has one passenger, the tiny female nucleus. The sperm arrives in a small rowing boat (his tail), which he leaves behind when he climbs aboard. He finds the nucleus, they unite with each other, and as the boat continues on its voyage the resulting *zygote* lives on the store of food with which it is loaded, growing bigger till it occupies the whole boat, and there is no food left.

"By the fifth day after conception, the fertilized ovum, now a mass of dividing cells, should arrive inside the womb. After the fifth day, it gets another name. Now it is the *blastocyst*—the *blast* part comes from a Greek word mean-

35

ing a 'bud' or 'shoot,' and the *cyst* means 'a kind of swelling.' We shall soon see why it gets this name.

"It may seem confusing that the new being changes its name so often. The sperm and ovum join to form the *zygote*. A few days later the *zygote* becomes the *blastocyst*. And there are more changes to come. A week or so later— or two weeks after conception—the blastocyst becomes the *embryo*. Six weeks after that—or two months after conception—the embryo becomes the *fetus*. Are all these names really necessary? Yes, they are useful because they describe different stages in development—just as the child after birth is first an infant, then a toddler, then a preschool child, then a child of grade-school age, then an early adolescent, then a late adolescent, then a young adult.

"Arrived in the womb, the developing new life is confronted with a crisis. It has run out of its food supply and must find a new source within a few days if it it to survive. Another way of putting this is to say that the boat must stop floating about, and go ashore so that it can take on further provisions.

"This is just what it does. It chooses a likely spot on the inside surface of the womb and, almost literally drops its anchor. Now we can understand the name blastocyst—a bud or root goes out and digs in to the wall of the womb. This is sometimes called the *trophoblast*—the *tropho* part of the word is from a Greek word meaning 'nourishment' or 'food.' In plain English, it can be called the food sprout.

"What we have described so far should make one point very clear. The being in your womb is not part of your body. This is never true at any time. It is *within* you, but not a part *of* you. Some embryologists tell us that, when it tries to dig in to the wall of the womb, the mother at first treats it as a parasite, an invader almost, and tries to fight it off.

Perhaps this has a value—a blastocyst too weak to develop into a healthy baby is unable to establish itself on the inner surface of the womb. It is estimated that about a quarter of all blastocysts fail to dig in, and are lost.

"As soon as the food sprout has its root down, it begins to draw nourishment from the rich lining of the womb (the *endometrium*), with its plentiful supply of blood, which would pass out in the menstrual flow later if pregnancy didn't occur. At the point of contact between the mother and her possible future child, a special organ, like a pancake, takes shape, and is called the *placenta* (from a Greek word meaning 'flat cake').

"We use two names to describe this process of digging in to the wall of the womb. One is *implantation*, which conveys the idea of a plant taking root in the soil. The other is *nidation*, which means 'making a nest'—setting up a safe place where new life can grow and develop. Both words have the same meaning, and either can be used.

"Only six or seven days have passed, but a great deal is now happening. Three different processes are taking place in the mass of dividing cells. The first I have already described—the setting up of the lifeline through the placenta, which enables a food supply (necessary chemicals for continuing life and growth) to be obtained from the mother's bloodstream, and waste materials to be disposed of or dumped into it. However, notice that the mother's blood as such doesn't enter the quite separate bloodstream of the embryo or fetus.

"A good way to picture this is to think of two separate railroad lines, not at all connected with each other, but both including a section of line that runs into the same station with a platform between them. When the freight cars of the first railroad come in to the station, a staff of

37

porters quickly unload whatever goods have been consigned to the second railroad and carry them across the platform to be loaded on to the other railroad's freight cars. This process works both ways, so that a continous exchange of freight is taking place between the two railroads, though the cars of one never run on the lines of the other. This complete separation of the two bloodstreams again emphasizes the fact that the life developing within the mother is quite separate and distinct from her own life.

"The railroad station where all this goes on is the placenta. This organ has also another function. It deals not only with the exchange of freight but also sets up a signaling system to send messages to the mother's body as well as to the developing embryo. The most important message is conveyed by a chemical which the placenta produces. It is the hormone called *progesterone,* which the mother also produces, and which controls the state of the lining of her womb, getting it ready for a possible conception every month. When a woman's progesterone supply drops, the womb lining shreds away, and her menstrual period starts. This must not happen during pregnancy, because it could cast off the growing embryo. So the excess progesterone from the placenta signals to her to keep up the rich blood supply in the inner surface of her womb, and the result is that she normally has no more monthly periods while the pregnancy lasts.

"I said there were three different operations going on, but I have so far described only one of them. The second is the development of the 'bag of waters' called the *amnion,* a sort of balloon which gradually fills with water so that the developing embryo can float freely inside it. Again this emphasizes the separateness of the developing new life. The fetus will grow till it completely fills the mother's womb, yet it will never be in direct contact with her body, but within a separate capsule of its own. Only in the process of birth will the baby for the first time directly touch the mother's body.

"The third process is the continuing development of the body that is to be nourished through the placenta and protected within the amnion. This is very complex, and all I need to do is to give you a general outline. You may in fact be thinking that I have already gone into unnecessary details, but you will realize later that this is not so. Everything I have explained will be necessary for our later discussion.

"Somewhere in the second or third week after conception, the point comes when *twinning* takes place, if it does at all. I am referring only to identical twins, which result from the embryo at a very early stage dividing into two. There is no need to go into technical details about this—only to point out that unless the splitting off happens at this point, it could not possibly happen afterward.

"The rest of the growing process, up to birth, is divided into two separate stages, the special names for which I have already mentioned. The name *embryo* (in Greek it means 'something that grows inside') is used to describe the new life from the end of the second week to the end of the eighth week. After that, we call it the fetus. The distinction usually made between these two stages is that the embryo is busily producing, in simple form, all the essential organs and systems of its body. By the end of two months after conception, this has been done, and after that, development means only the finishing and perfecting of the organs and a steady increase in size. The fetus is just the embryo grown bigger, more complete, and getting better and better equipped to survive outside the mother's body.

"The rate at which the embryo builds the little body may seem surprising until we remember that the chicken in the egg is complete, ready to break out and stand on its own feet, in just three weeks. A human body is of course much more complicated; yet at the end of one month, though it is less than half an inch long, the embryo has a head with eyes, ears, and the beginning of a brain; it has a simple digestive system, kidneys, and liver; a heart that beats and a bloodstream of its own; and there are bulges in the places where the arms and legs will soon grow.

"By the end of the eighth week, when the embryo changes its name and becomes a fetus, it is one inch long, and now has full arms and legs, with well-formed fingers and toes. The brain is at work, because electrical activity can be detected by a machine doctors use for this purpose. It is sensitive to touch—if tickled on the nose it will turn its head away!

"After twelve weeks the fetus has grown to three and a half inches. It can now move about vigorously in its water-filled capsule, and the mother should soon be able to feel it kicking. Our grandmothers called this *quickening,* because they thought there was a point at which the fetus suddenly came to life and started moving like a person waking out of sleep. But we now know it has been moving before, though not vigorously enough for the mother to be aware of it.

"Now that we have a fairly clear picture of what happens inside a woman's body during pregnancy, we are ready to consider what is involved in cutting off the process of growth of the embryo or fetus. This is what abortion means—the ending of the new life by its coming out of the womb before it can develop further. The word has come to be used also in a wider context. For example, when one of the moon flights ran into trouble the decision was made to abort the mission.

"We must distinguish between two kinds of abortion—spontaneous and induced. The spontaneous kind happens of its own accord, without any action on the part of the woman. We often call this a miscarriage. The induced kind is the result of deliberate intervention, brought about by the woman or by someone else because the pregnancy is not desired.

"Spontaneous abortion can take place at any point. As we have already seen, it is thought that about one-quarter of all zygotes are lost—the floating boat containing the united sperm and ovum nucleus never gets ashore, and is 'lost at sea.' Also, in some cases the blastocyst, although it starts to dig in, gets pushed off by the wall of the womb and is washed away in a menstrual period before the signal gets through to stop it.

"There are also cases where the embryo doesn't develop normally, because of some weakness, some breakdown in development, or through an illness. The new life comes to an end by death, and the boat loses its anchorage on the beachhead and is washed out to sea. At the embryo stage, the woman would probably be unaware of this kind of miscarriage. The embryo is so tiny that its death and departure would probably go unnoticed.

"The fetus also can get into trouble. It can sicken and die inside the womb and, for one reason or another, be washed out or pushed out. The woman would of course be aware of this, if only because her periods are resumed; although occasional unscheduled bleeding during pregnancy doesn't necessarily mean that the fetus is being lost.

"As we move further and further along in the development of the fetus, we reach a point at which we no longer use the word 'miscarriage.' At the stage at which it would be possible for the fetus to live outside the womb, we speak of a premature delivery. Legally a miscarriage used to mean spontaneous abortion up to the twenty-eighth week, or if the fetus weighed less than a thousand grams (two pounds, three ounces). After that, the fetus was said in law to be viable, able to survive outside the womb. This remains the legal definition, although nowadays, medical skill is able to make survival possible at a much earlier stage in the pregnancy.

"It is doubtful whether we would want to prevent spontaneous abortion even if we could. It represents nature's way of discarding abnormal, weak, or diseased fetuses, which would have poor chances of survival anyway. It used to be believed that miscarriages were often caused by accidents, straining, or shock; but this view is no longer accurate. 'You can't shake a good fetus loose as easily as that,' as one medical authority put it.

"Now we are ready to focus our attention on induced abortion, which is what you are really concerned about. We used to divide induced abortion into two kinds—therapeutic and criminal or legal and illegal. But with advances in medical skill and changes in the law and its enforcement, these terms have come to have uncertain meanings. It would be outside my province as a physician to deal with the question of what is legal, or what should be legal.

"Inducing an abortion means getting two things done. The life of the embryo or fetus must be ended, and its remains must be removed from the womb. These objects must be accomplished if at all possible without injury to the woman.

"The methods of producing abortion will depend on the stage the pregnancy has reached. No known method can reach the floating mass of developing cells during the week following conception. But as soon as the blastocyst tries to attach itself to the wall of the womb, steps can be taken to defeat it. For example, one method of birth control used by some women is the I.U.C.D. (intrauterine contraceptive device), popularly known as the 'loop.' This is a kind of coiled spring made of plastic, which is put into the womb and left there. Medical authorities differ about how it works; but one theory is that it prevents a blastocyst from taking root so that the developing cluster of cells can get no further food supply, and its growth comes to a stop.

"The contraceptive 'pill,' as it has come to be called, has a somewhat similar effect. Taken for twenty-eight consecutive days, it cancels out any signals that may be given by a blastocyst to stop the next menstrual period.

"Experiments are now going on with a morning-after pill that can be taken by a woman following intercourse when she fears it may possibly lead to an undesired pregnancy. This is likewise designed to prevent the fertilized ovum, if there is one, from taking root in the womb.

"Once implantation has taken place, and the embryo has rooted itself securely in the wall of the womb, more determined efforts must be made to get rid of it. External methods such as hot baths, violent exercise, or jumping from a height, are seldom effective, even when they are persisted in to the point of harming the mother. I know of one case in which the pregnant woman in desperation jumped off a cliff. She broke both legs and suffered other injuries—but the pregnancy was not affected at all.

"Chemicals and drugs are no better. All sorts of stories go around about what you can take to 'bring on your periods.' These concoctions are either ineffective or dangerous. Some of the drugs are poisonous, and the only conditions under which they would work would be by killing the fetus while the mother, better able to tolerate the poison, managed to survive. It is folly to take such risks.

"Abortions performed by physicians are done nowadays primarily by operative procedures. Under proper medical supervision, these are normally safe and effective. The same procedures, performed under other conditions, may be neither safe nor effective.

"Almost all abortions involve reaching the inside of the womb through the vagina and the cervix. The cervix, although it has a narrow opening through which the tiny sperms can easily penetrate, has to have this passage greatly widened before the interior of the womb can be reached. Widening the passage does no harm if it is done properly, because this happens naturally when a child is born. Instruments are used by doctors for this purpose; in difficult cases thin strips of surgical gauze are pushed into the womb and left there overnight. This causes the muscles of the womb to contract, which opens up the cervix in about twelve hours. A more recent method is to dilate the cervix by electrical vibration. In these and later operations, of course, the woman is given a suitable anesthetic to eliminate pain.

"Once the cervix is open, several procedures can be used. In some cases opening the cervix alone is enough to start labor, so that the fetus is naturally pushed out of the womb. The most common procedure until recently, however, was what is called D and C, which stands for dilation and currettage. The *curette* (the French word for "scraper') is a surgical instrument made of metal and rather like a tiny rake or hoe. It is passed repeatedly into the womb and used to scrape the wall thoroughly, which pulls off the lining to which the embryo is attached. Of course, the embryo itself

44

dies, and the physician alternates the use of the curette with that of forceps which pull out everything in the womb till it is finally empty and scraped clean. A skilled physician can do this without damage to the woman—in unskilled hands it is dangerously easy to rip through the womb itself as well as the lining, which could have fatal results.

"Another recent method of abortion, developed first in Russia, is now being used in this country. Once the cervix has been dilated, an open tube, attached at the other end to a vacuum pump, is pushed into the womb. When the pump is turned on, it sucks out the fetus, pulls the placenta up by the roots, and empties the womb in about two minutes. This method is considered to be highly effective and is being more and more widely used.

Both D and C and the suction method are effective only during the first three months of pregnancy. After that, the size of the fetus makes it difficult to operate the curette, and the danger of serious bleeding is very much increased. Doctors don't like to perform abortions at all after about twelve weeks of pregnancy. If they must, the traditional methods have been to open up the cervix and hope that labor contractions would begin; to push rubber tubes and other types of catheters into the womb, which tends to cause irritation and provoke the muscles to try to push them out, thus dislodging the fetus at the same time; or to break the bag of waters (amnion) surrounding the fetus, causing it to die and be pushed out.

"In advanced pregnancy, a kind of Caesarean operation has sometimes been performed—opening up the womb through the abdomen, removing the fetus, and sewing up the womb again. This is called hysterotomy (not to be confused with hysterectomy) and is simply an earlier form of what we call Caesarean section—making an incision in the womb and bringing the baby out.

"A more recent technique has been to draw out some of the amniotic water with a hollow needle and replace it with an equal amount of concentrated salt solution. Adding very strong salt concentrations kills the fetus, and in about twenty hours labor pains begin; it is pushed, dead, out of the womb. This method has been used successfully from the tenth to the twenty-fourth week of pregnancy.

"Not much need be said about the methods of unskilled abortionists. The most common procedure, after opening the cervix, was to use sharp or pointed instruments—knitting needles, pieces of wire from coat hangers, hatpins, and the like—to pierce the bag of waters and destroy the fetus. The danger of introducing infection or of poking the instrument right through the womb was very great. The other method was to use a syringe to squirt a solution of soap, salt, or disinfectant into the womb. The idea was that these irritating chemicals would cause the womb to start contractions and force the fetus out. What sometimes happened was that air or fluid under pressure was forced into a vein and passed into the woman's bloodstream—a great danger, resulting sometimes in death.

"As a result of this discussion, you should now clearly understand what abortion means. Let me, in conclusion, emphasize three points.

"First, if abortion is performed by a qualified physician in a hospital or clinic provided with the means of dealing with a possible emergency, it can be carried out with a high level of safety. Studies of death rates when abortions take place under these conditions show that the risks are relatively slight. Modern methods are effective, and anesthetics prevent pain. Recovery is quite rapid—unless there are complications, one night in a hospital bed is enough, and even that is not considered really necessary. The operation is quickly performed, and most women will be back to normal health in a few days.

"Second, the fact must be faced that what abortion means is the killing of the embryo or fetus. The use of this unpleasant word is avoided in most discussions of the subject. Even in medical books the writers speak of 'evacuating the contents of the uterus' or 'removing the fetal tissue.' But it is simply dishonest to evade the fact that the embryo or fetus is alive when the operation begins and dead when it is over. Just what has been killed is a perplexing question, which I am not competent to discuss. But it is only realistic to acknowledge that inducing abortions is an unpleasant business, and all sensitive people wish it didn't have to be done. I don't think this means it *shouldn't* be done, but I think it should never be done lightly or without very good reason, and we should all fervently hope for the day when it will no longer be necessary.

"The third point arises out of the other two. Everything about abortion emphasizes that if it has to be done, it should be done as early as possible in the pregnancy. Doctors are very emphatic about this. It is much less complicated to perform an abortion at eight or ten weeks, than later. Not only the difficulty of the operation but also its danger to the woman increases rapidly after about ten or twelve weeks. And this goes for the life within the womb also. Whatever conclusion we reach about the value of the life, if it has to be taken, it is merciful to take it soon, during an early stage of development, when there is little sensitivity to pain and death. Thank you."

Cynthia Boyd rises.

"Thank you indeed, Dr. Archer, for a very full, clear presentation. This will be very helpful to us. And we appreciate particularly the seriousness with which you have treated the subject.

"Now, ladies, I want to give you a chance to ask a few questions—but please, only a few, and make them as brief as possible. Our time is limited."

"I want to express my personal thanks, Dr. Archer. I learned some things I never knew before. One was about how the embryo and fetus are completely separate from the mother's body. Yet when the campaign for free abortion was going on, I often heard speakers say that all it meant was removing a part of the woman's body, and the woman should have the right to decide that this should be done, just as she can decide to have her appendix removed."

"All I can do is to repeat what I have said. You could claim, perhaps, that the ovum was once part of the woman's body. But once it has been released from the ovary, it floats freely and has its own independent life. Once it has been fertilized, the zygote is made up equally of what has been contributed by the man and what has been contributed by the woman; so you could say that the man had an equal right to decide what should happen to it! Of course, it is the woman exclusively who provides it with the nourishment necessary for its growth. But this certainly does not make it a part of her body. As you probably know, a zygote has been taken from a woman's body and given nourishment artificially, continuing its growth for a time. That's what they mean when they talk of the possibility of test-tube babies. No doubt we shall be able, someday, to create the conditions necessary for babies to be grown outside the womb; and to transfer them, if necessary, from the womb of one mother to the womb of another.

"I know that some people—occasionally even doctors— have been guilty of making statements of the kind you mention. I can only state emphatically that such statements are inaccurate."

"Doctor, I was very much impressed by what you said about how quickly the unborn baby develops. If it has all its essential organs at the end of eight weeks, why does it have to stay in the womb so much longer? It would be very much more convenient for us women if our babies could be born when they're a couple of inches long"

"Yes, that would be a good idea, wouldn't it? You may know that this does happen for some animals—kangaroos, for example. The tiny baby is born, and climbs up into the mother's pouch, where he does the rest of his growing until he is able to venture off on his own. Birds, of course, don't carry their young inside their bodies at all.

"Why do we humans do so? Well, it just must have been the most convenient way. You know, of course, that we can take care of premature babies now much earlier than was once possible—they can occasionally survive as early as twenty-four weeks. The nurses say it seems strange that we use medical skill to save the lives of some babies and to take the lives of others, of exactly the same age. I'm afraid this is true. But we doctors don't make that decision. It is the mothers who decide—some want their babies, others don't. The state now gives them the right to act according to their personal wishes."

"Doctor Archer, I hope you won't mind this question. You have been quite frank with us in telling us that abortion is taking life. You mentioned that at eight weeks the embryo —or fetus—will turn away its head if its nose is tickled. That must mean it can feel. Well, carrying out an abortion goes a long way beyond tickling its nose. Does it suffer pain like we would do? You also talked about giving the mother something to prevent pain. Do you give the fetus an anesthetic, too?"

"Your question deserves an honest answer. There can be no doubt that the fetus experiences pain. But it would hardly be like your own experience. The nervous system and brain of the fetus are in a much more elementary state of development than ours are. And most methods of abortion are very swiftly performed. Death comes to the fetus without warning, and probably as swiftly as when a man is fatally hit by an automobile. The salt solution method, used with a more developed fetus, is something else again because death would not necessarily be instantaneous. No, it is not customary to give the fetus an anesthetic.

"I don't resent your question. I have had it asked before. I must repeat what I said earlier. Abortion is something no sensitive person feels comfortable about, and we wish it didn't have to be done. But I believe there are situations in which it is justified, as the lesser of two evils."

"Sorry, there isn't time for any more questions. Dr. Archer, you have been most helpful to us. We are deeply grateful. And now, ladies, we shall take a ten-minute break before our next session."

The Abortion Conference, Session 2— "Attitudes to Abortion, Past and Present"

"When we planned this conference, we decided that we ought to take a good look at the way in which other people, in other times as well as in our own, have thought about abortion. So we have asked Dr. Arthur Ferguson to do this for us. Dr. Ferguson is a professor at Westford College, where he teaches social ethics. He has recently made a special study of this subject. We have asked him to present to us a short history of attitudes to abortion in the past and a discussion of present attitudes.

"Dr. Ferguson, welcome to our conference. We are very grateful to have you with us."

"Thank you, Mrs. Boyd. I am afraid you have been altogether too generous in introducing me. I can't claim to be an expert on this subject. I teach social ethics, and of course that puts abortion in my field. But until the big public discussion about the new law got started, I hadn't studied it very seriously. Then my students began to embarrass me by asking me questions I couldn't answer, so I had to dig more deeply than I have ever done before.

"In a conference of this kind, you certainly don't need a great deal of detail about abortion in the past. What we are concerned about is the present situation and how best to meet it. However, I think it's hard to understand the present unless you can relate it to the past, so I believe we shall find it helpful to begin by looking briefly at the historical picture.

"Back in 1955, an anthropologist named George Devereux published a major study of abortion among primitive peoples. His book covers a great deal of ground. It would be difficult even to summarize his conclusions, and I'm not going to try. What is interesting for us, however, is to discover that abortion has been practiced in almost all human communities. It isn't just a problem of our modern era. It has been a universal human problem. References to it have been found throughout the whole span of recorded human history, going as far back as ancient China forty-six hundred years ago.

"Our own Western society, as we know, had its roots in three main cultural sources—those of the Greeks, of the Hebrews, and of the Romans. It seems that abortion was pretty freely practiced in the Greco-Roman world, but the Old Testament has only one reference to it, suggesting that it was *not* common among the Hebrews.

"Let's begin with the Greeks. Plato in his *Republic* and again in *The Laws* refers to abortion as a means of controlling population in the ideal state; but he also suggests sending surplus citizens abroad to found new colonies, so he wasn't going to depend on abortion for this purpose. Aristotle in his *Politics* also suggests that a couple who already have as many children as they can manage may resort to abortion, but he is careful to say that this is justified only in the early period of pregnancy—we shall return to this point in a minute. Hippocrates, "the Father of Medicine," seems to have been opposed to abortion. The famous Hippocratic Oath, still taken by physicians today, includes the pledge: 'I will not give to a woman an abortifacient pessary. In purity and holiness I will guard my life and my art.'

"In practice population control was not a significant reason for abortion in the ancient world. Soranus, the greatest of the Greek gynecologists, reports that abortion was resorted to for three main reasons—to remove the evidence of adultery, to maintain feminine beauty, and to safeguard the life of a woman whose womb was too small to carry a child.

"Among the wealthier Roman families, according to a report of Ambrose, Bishop of Milan, abortion was used to keep down the number of heirs among whom the family fortune would have to be divided. Whatever the reasons, we gain the impression that abortion was quite common among the Romans. Seneca even went out of his way to praise his mother for having allowed him to be born.

"What methods of abortion were used in those days? Soranus gives us a list including special drugs, suppositories followed by shaking, vigorous walking, lifting heavy weights, bathing in special concoctions, applying hot poultices. Modern knowledge suggests that most of these would not have worked. Soranus also mentions sharp instruments, but disapproves of them. In practice, however, they probably proved to be the only effective methods.

"It is always dangerous to judge social customs in any culture either by the opinions of its distinguished men or by the practices of the upper classes. We have seen that Plato and Aristotle advocated abortion for population control. But we need to remember that in the ancient world generally and often among primitive people, unwanted children were killed outright at birth or exposed—abandoned and left to die. The Roman law, indeed, expressly gave the father the power of life and death over his own children; and his wife could only be punished for having an abortion when it was carried out without his consent. It seems likely, therefore, that in these ancient societies the real reason for most abortions was not population control, but the concealment of pregnancies that were the result of illicit sex relations.

"One of our best sources of information about what was going on lies in the early Christian writings and the fact that they so often condemned their pagan neighbors for both abortion and infanticide. This would not have been necessary if these practices had not been fairly common. The Christian Church from the beginning regarded abortion as a serious sin. The *Teaching of the Twelve Apostles,* one of the earliest Christian writings outside the New Testament, said plainly, 'You shall not slay a child by abortion. You shall not kill what is generated.' Similar passages appear in other early Christian writings. The *Apocalypse of Peter* speaks of women 'who have caused their children to be born untimely and have corrupted the work of God who created them.' This theme occurs again and again—life is given directly by God, and must not be destroyed. This attitude contrasted sharply with the widespread pagan view that the lives of people of low degree—especially of slaves and of infants—were not of any special value.

"What about the Hebrew attitude? The only reference to abortion in the Old Testament is in Ex. 21:22, which refers to the man who accidentally hurts a woman so that he terminates her pregnancy. The implication is that *deliberate* termination of pregnancy would be unthinkable. The divine commandment to 'be fruitful and multiply' gave the Hebrews a profound respect for child life, which they considered as a special gift from God. The high Christian value placed on early life undoubtedly had its roots in this Hebrew attitude. The absence of direct references to abortion in the New Testament strongly suggests that it was not practiced to any significant degree in the Jewish community. It was only later, when Christians lived in closer contact with the pagan community in the Roman Empire, that vigorous attacks on abortion began to be made.

"We should now look at some of the ideas about abortion which were expressed in ancient times and which had a great influence on later thinking. Probably the most important one was the view of Aristotle that in the early life of the unborn child it had first a 'vegetable soul,' its existence was like that of a plant without movement or sensation. Later, it developed an 'animal soul' and could now feel and move. Finally it came to possess a human or 'rational soul.' Linked with these concepts is his view that at a certain point in growth—forty days for the male and ninety for the female—the fetus develops 'distinct parts,' suggesting that this is the time when sensation begins. These concepts played a very important role in later religious controversies about the unborn child. Aristotle suggested that abortion before there is 'sensation and life' may be permitted; after that point it is not permitted.

"The Hebrews took a rather different view. Based on the account of Adam's creation, when God breathed into him the breath of life, and he became a 'living soul,' the theory was developed that only when the child was born and took his first breath, did he become truly human and possess a soul. This idea enabled some major Jewish authorities to justify abortion in situations where the mother's life was in danger. Generally speaking, Jewish tradition has allowed abortion only in cases of medical necessity.

"Since Western culture has been shaped largely by Christian teaching, we must take a careful look at the Catholic attitude to abortion. John T. Noonan, Jr. has given us an excellent summary of the history of Catholic doctrine in his book *The Morality of Abortion,* and he makes it clear that the Catholic Church has never departed significantly from the view that abortion must be regarded as a form of homicide or murder. As you all know, this extreme position has produced increasingly violent controversy in recent years, especially the Catholic view that it is wrong to take the life of an unborn child even to save the life of the mother.

"There were, however, periods in Christian history when the Catholic Church was divided about its teaching on abortion. The main difference of opinion went back to the question that had been raised by Aristotle—whether there is a time early in pregnancy when the fetus has no truly human soul. There were many discussions about the 'unformed fetus' and the 'formed fetus.' Augustine, the greatest of the early fathers of the Church, said, 'there cannot yet be said to be a live soul in a body that lacks sensation.' He was not saying that early abortion was not sinful—even contraception was sinful in his eyes—but he *was* saying that early abortion can't be murder if the fetus is not fully alive at the time.

"This distinction between the formed and the unformed fetus kept reappearing. It was impossible to settle the matter, for two reasons. First, in those days there was very little clear knowledge about unborn life. We must remember that until the microscope came along nothing was known about the existence of the sperm and ovum, and

56

doctors at that time were generally very ignorant about how our bodies worked—even the circulation of the blood was not understood. So people were naturally confused about just when, and how, the fetus 'came alive.' Some followed Aristotle's forty-day rule. Others thought that 'quickening,' when the woman felt the child moving within her, was the decisive sign.

"The other problem was even more complicated. It was the question of what is called 'ensoulment'—just when does the fetus receive a human soul? There were many theories and many arguments, but, of course, there was absolutely no scientific way of proving which view was the correct one. The only point on which everyone could agree was that once the fetus *had* received its rational soul, destroying it was a form of murder. Before that, destroying it was still sinful, but it was a less serious sin.

"The best way to understand Roman Catholic moral teaching on this subject is to remember that the church regarded every kind of interference with nature's process of reproduction as sinful. But the further along you go in the reproductive process, the greater the sin becomes. They started with contraception—it was sinful to prevent conception. It was more sinful to destroy the new life after conception but before it had received a human soul. After ensoulment, abortion was very sinful, and indeed a form of murder. But to kill the child after birth—infanticide—was worst of all.

"This rising scale of sinfulness is reflected in the penalties which the church imposed on those who were guilty of the various sins. But the whole system got into trouble because nobody could distinguish clearly between the second and the third degrees because of the disagreement about when the soul appeared.

"The issue of ensoulment continued to be argued back and forth, and it was not finally settled until the Second Vatican Council, when the decision was made, in the light of modern scientific knowledge, that conception is the point at which a distinctive new human life begins and that this must be viewed as the time of ensoulment. The Council said, 'life from its conception is to be guarded with the greatest care. Abortion and infanticide are horrible crimes.' The Council's view was made official Catholic doctrine by Pope Paul in December, 1965.

"What about the Prostestant Church? Luther and Calvin were as strongly opposed to abortion as were the Catholics, and the Lutheran Church has maintained this conservative position until very recently. The American Lutheran Conference adopted a resolution in 1952 which said, 'abortion must be regarded as the destruction of a living being, and except as a medical measure to save the mother's life will not be used by a Christian to avoid an unwanted birth.' The Lambeth Conference in 1930, representing Episcopal bishops throughout the world, had already passed a resolution which said, 'the Conference further records its abhorrence of the sinful practice of abortion.' These two statements probably fairly represent the attitudes adopted, until quite recently, by the more conservative Protestant groups. The other Protestant Churches, as far as I can discover, tended to take no formal position on the subject. They left each individual pastor and member free to follow his or her own conscience.

"In recent years, however, many of the Protestant Churches and the more liberal Jewish groups have adopted much more liberal attitudes. Official statements to this effect have been issued by such bodies as the American Baptist Convention, the Lutheran Church in America, the Presbyterian Church in the U. S., the United Church of Christ, The United Methodist Church, and The United Presbyterian Church in the U.S.A.

"Apart from religious opinion, the best way to judge public attitudes to abortion is through the laws passed on the subject. I shall not say anything about that, however, because I understand that your next speaker will be dealing with it.

"Up to now we have been talking about official attitudes to abortion. But it would be quite misleading to think that theologians and lawmakers had the power to decide what ordinary people did. Throughout the history of our Western world, while the Church thundered against abortion, abortions went on being performed. You could call them immoral and make them illegal, but you couldn't stop them. Why? Because the human dilemmas in which women found themselves drove them to seek abortion whether it was moral or not, whether it was legal or not. Theories about abortion were evolved by men, and usually by celibate priests. Laws on abortion were almost invariably made by men. But the reality of abortion was something that concerned women, and they were hardly ever consulted. As someone has neatly put it, if men had been exposed to unwanted pregnancies, they would have passed very different laws about abortion.

"So illegal abortion has always been practiced, and no nation has ever been able to suppress it. Theory and practice have never succeeded in keeping in step with one another. And now in our own time, the conflict between them has burst out into the open with explosive force.

"I want to spend the rest of my time talking about the dramatic change of attitude we are witnessing today. I think we shall understand this much more clearly in the light of our brief historical survey, because the present campaign for liberalized abortion is in part a violent protest against what has happened in the past.

"The abortion controversy in our time must be seen as a product of what we call the sexual revolution. Our whole culture has been kept for so long in a state of unhealthy sexual repression that, with the sudden removal of these controls, we are unable to cope with the resulting situation, because we have as yet no clear guidelines. In this confused state, we are apt to swing wildly from one extreme of opinion to the other. We have taken a leap from silence about sex to loud talk about sex, from extremes of sexual privacy to extremes of sexual publicity, from condemning adultery to commending it. And in our approach to abortion, we have likewise moved, with startling rapidity, from strict suppression to open approval.

"The speed at which all of this has happened may quite possibly represent an all-time record for rapid change in the field of social ethics. The pace has been so fast that strict abortion laws had hardly been changed to liberal laws before the demand was made to repeal all laws and to treat abortion as a purely private matter.

"This sweeping pace of change has been brought about by an unusual, perhaps unique, convergence of forces and circumstances. The main ones can be identified as four pressure groups or lobbies, as follows:

"1. *The Sexual Freedom Lobby.* For a long time radical groups have been pressing in our culture for changes in our standards of sexual behavior. They began with the free-love cult of half a century ago and first attacked our traditional standards of premarital chastity. Now, having made considerable headway in that direction, the attack has shifted to our traditional standards of sexual fidelity in marriage. A central plank in the platform of the sexual freedom movement has been the assumption that scientific contraception now enables us to avoid undesired pregnancy, and that this makes it no longer necessary to confine sexual intercourse to marriage. Unfortunately, however, this has been a premature claim because our available contraceptives are still far from fool-proof; and the best of them, the pill, has been in disfavor lately because of its possibly serious side effects. The promoters of sexual freedom therefore saw in legalized abortion an accepted backup resource for contraceptive failures and advocated the removal of all legal controls which prevented this.

"2. *The Population Control Lobby.* The ominous shadow of overpopulation now threatens our world. Until recently this seemed to apply only to the teeming millions in the less developed countries. But now the issue is seen as threatening our own country too, and many are in favor of a zero rate of population increase. Abroad, the most successful program of population control is unquestionably that of Japan, which has been based on the availability of legal abortion to any woman. In the United States, contraception as the basis of population control has certainly not been abandoned, but many people feel that it should be reinforced by making abortion available upon request. These people, who include government officials, have supported the liberal abortion campaign.

"3. *The Women's Liberation Lobby.* Throughout most of human history, women have been treated as second-class citizens. Their demand for emancipation has gradually won for them the right to vote, the right to higher education, the right to gainful employment, and other privileges. But a number of stubborn pockets of masculine resistance have still to be reduced, one of which concerns the sexual rights of women. Essential among these is the right of the woman to decide for herself how she will use her sexuality, and particularly her procreative powers. The women's liberation movement has taken the view that if a woman finds that she has conceived and does not wish to bear a child, she should have the right to demand medical termination of the pregnancy. The movement therefore has declared the right of every woman to abortion on request to be one of its major goals.

"4. *The Medical Lobby.* Physicians have traditionally tended to oppose abortion as being contrary to their basic goal of maintaining and saving life. But a striking change has taken place in the past few years, and many powerful medical groups have come out in favor of liberalized abortion. The reasons for this about-face include the wish to end the illegal traffic in abortion which has sometimes led to serious illness and death, the development of new methods which make abortion a much safer procedure than it has been in the past, and a realization that many women seek abortion for good reasons and that they should no longer be denied dependable medical service.

"These four groups, with support from some lawyers, social scientists, and clergymen, have merged rapidly into a very powerful pressure group for the policy of making abortion easier to get. Against the campaign they mounted, there has until recently been little organized resistance. The Catholics have stood their ground, but their declared position is considered to be so extreme that they have found little support; and a large number of Protestants and Jews gave up their traditional conservative position and went over to the liberal side. The general public was faced with a hot controversy over a very complex subject about which most people knew very little. So for a time the movement for free abortion swept everything before it and achieved unexpectedly easy victories.

"From the point of view of social ethics, which is my subject, it seems that the arguments which won these victories have had very little to do with the real issue of abortion. As I said before, the issues have rather been sexual freedom, population control, women's rights, and changing concepts of the scope of medicine. Very seldom have the people involved in the controversy sat down to ask themselves and one another, honestly and objectively, what it means for a highly civilized culture to accept and approve the practice of ending the lives of millions of unborn human beings. There has been little or no attempt to define the conditions under which it can be considered morally right to terminate a pregnancy. In fact, the real question has been sidestepped by the argument that the woman has a right to make her own decision in consultation with her physician. Society has abdicated its responsibility for thinking through this maddeningly complicated question and turned it over to the woman and her doctor.

"Please don't misunderstand me. I am not saying that what has happened is all a mistake and that we must put the clock back. On balance, I think the situation we are in now is a little better than the one we were in before. We are giving the woman more freedom to choose. But we are doing little or nothing to help her in making that choice. We have simply turned our backs and left her to wrestle with it alone. Her doctor can do the abortion if she is clear in her mind and in her conscience that she wants it done. But her doctor has neither the time nor the training to help her decide what is ethically right for her in the light of the particular set of circumstances in which she is placed.

"You will understand from what I have just said why I am so glad that you have set up this conference. We are developing laws that give the woman greater freedom to choose abortion if she so decides. But who is going to help the woman to decide? She needs help—a lot of help. She not only has the right to choose but the right to be given all the support she needs in order to make the best and most responsible decision of which she is capable. I know this is what you ladies are concerned about, and I want to tell you that I commend you for accepting the responsibility to provide your sisters in trouble with all the assistance you can give them.

"Finally, I want to try to summarize the real dilemma with which abortion confronts us. It's a dilemma to which there is no simple answer. It's a dilemma in which there can be no general solution that can be applied to all cases, or even to certain types of cases. Every woman's situation is unique. Every case must be decided on its own merits, by balancing the issues and coming up with what seems to be the best plan for all concerned.

"I said for *all* concerned. Let me emphasize this as clearly and emphatically as I can—*there is no abortion situation in which only one person is involved.* There are sometimes many persons. That's what makes it so complicated.

"First, there is the fetus, the unborn life. The word 'person' isn't correct here, of course. We can argue and argue about what exactly the fetus is, just as the theologians argued about whether it had a soul or what kind of soul it had. We don't use the word 'soul' so much today. But the dilemma is still there. Is this a human being, or isn't it? It isn't a person, because it hasn't a name, an identity. It doesn't know other persons, and other persons don't know it. Yet it is in the process of becoming a person. If it is allowed to live, it will soon have a name and an identity and live a human life just as we are doing now. The decision we have to make is whether to let it become a person, or not.

"So we have to recognize that the fetus has rights that need to be considered. The trouble with the Catholic attitude to abortion, however, is that just about all the emphasis has been placed on the rights of the fetus. The rights of the fetus have been made so all-important that nobody else really matters much. Its mother, for instance, has to be prepared to die rather than to deny the fetus its rights, even though it would be almost a certainty that the fetus would die with her. The fetus has rights, yes. But not all the rights. Others have rights too.

"Today at last we have recognized the rights of the mother. She has the right to her own independent life. If the fetus, even innocently, is going to wreck her life by causing her death or ruining her health or unbalancing her mind or plunging her into misery or in some other way doing her grievous harm, then the rights of the fetus must be balanced against the rights of the mother.

"But the mother isn't the only person who has rights either. That's where the women's liberation movement goes to the other extreme. It talks about the woman having the absolute right to an abortion. But that's just as unbalanced as the Catholic Church talking about the absolute rights of the fetus to live. There are no absolute rights. There are many parties involved, not just the fetus and the mother.

"There is the father, for instance. After all, the fetus has two parents, and biologically it takes half of its endowment from each. I know that many men are quite indifferent about this. They have their fun, and they couldn't care less about what happens to their seed after they have sowed it. But some *do* care. And more *ought* to care in a responsible society.

"The family has rights, too. If the mother has other children, they are involved. If this fetus lives, it might mean disaster for the other children, because the resources just couldn't be stretched to meet the needs of all of them. If there is a chance that this will be a deformed or defective child, the burden of caring for that child may break down the family's means of coping with life and create havoc.

"Society also has rights. Parenthood never can be a private and personal matter. What the woman has to decide is whether she will allow a new member of the human race to join its fellows or close the door and deny it entrance. Society may not want new members, it may have more than enough already. Yet society always needs new people with high potential. If a woman decides to have an abortion, we have to recognize the possibility that when the surgeon takes his curette in his hand, he may be depriving the world of another Shakespeare or Beethoven or Einstein. This is a disturbing thought, yet it is a valid part of the maddeningly complicated equation.

"I have spoken of the dilemma with which abortion confronts us. Let me close by saying something about how we can begin to resolve that dilemma.

"The best solution of all will be to prevent situations arising that create the need for abortion. Many things can contribute to this—better sex education, more effective contraception, means by which any woman who has been exposed to the possibility of an unwanted pregnancy can prevent it from ever getting started. That may still be abortion, but Aristotle was right in principle when he took the view that the sooner this thing is done, the less ethically distasteful it will be. All these are practical possibilities. There are probably some others.

"Some people have been rather shocked to find women campaigning actively for the right to destroy the unborn life within them. They have seen this as a strange reversal of nature—mother-love so tragically twisted that a woman can seek the destruction of her own unborn child. I personally view this as an unjust and superficial judgment. The fact that a woman can reach this frame of mind is a sign not of her degeneration, but of her desperation. And we need to remember that it is always a man who got her into this condition, even if she encouraged him to do so.

"Yet there is profound truth in the fact that our human destiny depends absolutely on the willingness of women to become mothers—to conceive children, to nurture them within their bodies, to bear them, to raise them, and above all to love and cherish them. If we are mismanaging the business of motherhood today, this is a serious reflection on our society, and we must face it and develop a better policy. Men must do their part, and the indications are that in the future fathers will accept a major role in child rearing. But I am quite sure that if our society is going to develop a sound policy for parenthood and handle wisely the best interests of our future children, born and unborn, then the people we can trust to make that policy are the women, and especially the mothers in our midst.

"So, ladies, it's up to you! If we are to have a sound policy about abortion, *you* are the people we can trust to make it for us."

"We haven't much time left, but perhaps you have a question or two you are eager to ask Dr. Ferguson. Who will begin?"

"Dr. Ferguson, you mentioned the Catholic policy that a woman must die rather than have an abortion. But isn't there some way around this? I heard of a devout Catholic woman who was operated on when she was pregnant. In fact, I believe she had a hysterectomy."

"Yes, you are quite right. The Catholics have developed what they call the moral principle of the double effect. This means that if your *intention* is to do good and in the process you incidentally and unavoidably do evil at the same time, the evil can be overlooked. So far as abortion is concerned, it works this way. Suppose there is a malignancy in the womb, and the woman is pregnant. It would be evil for the doctor to kill the fetus deliberately. But operating to remove the cancer is doing good. This is the main effect that is intended. If this means removing the womb—hysterectomy—that would be permitted, even though as a secondary effect it causes the death of the fetus. I think this must have been what happened to the lady you heard about."

"Dr. Ferguson, you said we have turned our backs on the woman who has to decide whether or not to have an abortion. But what we have been campaigning for is that the question should be decided between the woman and her physician. Surely he is capable of dealing with her problem. Isn't abortion a medical matter really?"

"That's a tricky question, and I must watch my step. Maybe I should ask, Is there a doctor in the house? But let me give you a straight answer, which is not meant to cast any reflections upon our physicians—how would we ever manage without them?

"In terms of the operation which is necessary, yes, abortion is a medical matter. The physician is the expert who knows *how* to do it. But once the woman knows she is free to have an abortion if she wishes, her problem isn't *how* it will be done—she is willing to leave that to the doctor's technical skill, as she would if she needed to have her appendix removed.

"The woman's problem is *whether* she feels justified in taking the life of her unborn child. If her reason for doing this happens to be a medical one, then of course her doctor would be the right person to advise her. However, the overwhelming majority of abortions today are not sought for medical reasons, but for personal, social, economic reasons that have to do with the woman's life situation and not with her health. If the woman has the good fortune to have a physician who is trained in personal counseling and who can devote to her the several hours it may easily take to go into her situation in detail, all will be well. But to my knowledge, very few physicians are ready for that kind of involvement. Anyway, it wouldn't represent a wise use of the physician's time because we are desperately short of physicians. So I think the extensive counseling the woman often needs can more conveniently be given by someone else who has had special training for it. Unfortunately we have so far made no provision for this."

Cynthia Boyd comes to the podium. "I am sorry, ladies, but we just don't have time for any more questions. Immediately after our break, Dr. Lawrence Kolb will be speaking to us about the legal aspects of abortion. Once again, thank you very much, Dr. Ferguson. This session is now adjourned."

The Abortion Conference, Session 3– "The Liberalizing of Abortion: A World Perspective"

"Now we turn to the question of what the law says about abortion. It may seem to some of you that this will not be as interesting as the other lectures in our program. But the law of the land should be the voice of the people, and our planning committee was fully convinced that we must include this topic in our conference. We are all the more eager to do this since we have Dr. Lawrence Kolb in our community. He is, as you know, a professor in our law school here in the city.

"Most laymen and laywomen consider law to be a very dull subject, and I assure you I could make it so. However, I know you are not concerned with technicalities. You simply want a broad outline of what the law here and in other countries has to say about abortion. I will try to provide that outline.

"You are aware, of course, that the main purpose of laws is to prevent individuals from doing what the majority of the people consider to be wrong or undesirable. Wherever people live together in groups, they soon have to make rules of some kind to regulate their behavior. Otherwise, some individuals may soon begin to annoy or exploit or hurt others, and the peace and harmony of the community may be disturbed or even destroyed.

"A good deal of this controlling of people's behavior is achieved by customs, which decide what is done and what is not done in the community. Most of us have a healthy fear of offending others or making nuisances of ourselves, and this is usually enough to keep us in line. If that fails to work, it becomes necessary for us to be punished when we break the rules, so that it hurts enough to discourage us from doing it again. All parents have to use this kind of procedure in raising their children. What the law does is to use the power of punishment to deal with bad behavior in adults. One concept of law is to view it as a kind of parental discipline applied to the community as a whole.

"Historically, our legal system goes back to Roman times. In ancient Rome matters like abortion were settled within the family—which meant that the father was free to take the matter into his own hands. In fact, the Roman father had the power of life and death over his children, and he could insist that his wife abort a child he didn't want her to bear. Under these conditions, abortion could only be called a crime when a woman destroyed her unborn child without her husband's consent or against his wishes.

"In later Roman times, this unlimited power of the father was abolished by the Emperor Hadrian. But abortion continued to be practiced, especially by the aristocracy.

"It was Christianity that changed this attitude of indifference. As Christian power grew in the Roman Empire, the Church councils passed their own laws. One of the earliest of these laws excommunicated for life any woman who deliberately terminated a pregnancy. Throughout the history of the Church there were many controversies about abortion. The main disagreement was about when the unborn child received a human soul. Obviously, after that had happened, abortion became a more serious crime, deserving a more serious punishment. But abortion at any time was always considered wrong in Christian circles because it meant destroying a human, or potentially human, life given by God.

"In Western Europe generally, the law followed the general principle underlying English Common Law that pregnancy must not be interrupted after 'quickening,' and then only to save the life of the woman. The first abortion laws in the United States adopted this position. Little was known then about the growth of the unborn child within the womb. As knowledge increased, the state laws were changed after the middle of the nineteenth century to make abortion illegal at any stage of pregnancy. We could say that this was the position taken by abortion law generally in Christian countries at the beginning of the present century.

"We can best see the process of liberalizing abortion if we follow changes in the law through a series of steps, moving from the most conservative to the most liberal positions.

"1. *Abortion not permitted in any circumstances.* This was the traditional Catholic position. Abortion was not allowed even to save the life of the mother, although there were some ways of getting around this. Laws which absolutely prohibit abortion were until recently the general rule in Catholic countries and in most Moslem countries.

"2. *Abortion permitted only to save the mother's life.* This was the traditional Jewish and Protestant position, and it was the basis of law in most Protestant lands until the recent changes began to be made. The concept of therapeutic abortion had to be established on clear medical evidence that the woman's life would be in danger unless the pregnancy were terminated. This state of affairs didn't often occur, and consequently legal abortions of this kind were not often performed.

"3. *Abortion permitted to safeguard the mother's physical health.* Physicians were reluctant to declare that unless a woman patient had an abortion she would certainly die. It was easier, however, to predict that going ahead with the pregnancy would be injurious to her physical health. Up to the 1940s, quite a number of diseases were considered to justify therapeutic abortion—diseases especially of the heart, the stomach, the kidneys, the nerves, and the lungs, and such diseases as diabetes and cancer. The extra strain of pregnancy was judged to increase the danger of the disease. Nowadays, highly developed techniques of medical care can cut these risks to a minimum, and abortion on purely medical grounds is seldom considered to be really necessary.

"4. *Abortion permitted to safeguard the mother's mental health.* It was inevitable that in time therapeutic abortion should be extended to cover mental illness. This wider interpretation of the law came about in England as a result of a dramatic event. Dr. Alec Bourne, a physician, performed an abortion in 1938 on a fourteen-year-old girl who had been raped by several soldiers and was found to be pregnant. After performing the abortion, Dr. Bourne gave himself up to the police. The resulting trial was given a great deal of publicity. In the end, Dr. Bourne was acquitted. He had argued that the suffering this girl would have endured in bearing the child would have been as injurious to her health as a physical illness would have been. This famous court decision opened the door to a much wider interpretation of the law, both in England and in other countries.

"5. *Abortion permitted for social and economic reasons.* Once the law recognized that a woman under severe mental stress might have an abortion, it was natural that cases would arise where the cause of this mental stress was the wretched conditions in which the woman was living. It was the Scandinavian countries that first amended their laws in this direction. The first Pregnancy Act in Denmark, which went into operation in 1939, included *sociomedical* indications for abortion, and in 1946 Sweden also amended its laws to include sociomedical indications. These laws allowed the woman's general living condition to be taken into account—inadequate housing, extreme poverty, too many children already to enable her to be an effective mother, and so on. In other countries, social and economic circumstances tended more and more to be considered in relation to the woman's mental health, leading to more liberal interpretations of the existing law. The new British law of 1967 expressly covered social and economic factors by saying that 'account may be taken of the pregnant woman's actual or reasonably foreseeable environment.'

"6. *Abortion permitted after felonious conception.* This means that if the act of sexual intercourse that led to the pregnancy was a felony (a serious crime), abortion could be legal. The two felonies usually considered in this connection are rape and incest. We have seen that in the Alec Bourne case the girl he aborted had been raped. But this was an extreme case of a very young girl brutally assaulted by several soldiers. In acquitting Dr. Bourne the court didn't imply that any and every case of rape would automatically justify legal abortion. However, the Scandinavian laws did

74

from the beginning include criminal sexual acts as justifying abortion on what they called humanitarian grounds. These were included also in the model law drawn up in 1962 by the American Legal Institute—I'll say more about this in a moment.

"7. *Abortion permitted on eugenic grounds.* So far the reasons for abortion, legally allowed and being continuously liberalized, were concerned only with the welfare of the pregnant woman. This one, however, for the first time included the welfare of the unborn child. Again the Scandinavians were the first to include this indication in their abortion laws. The Danish law which took effect in 1939 included cases in which the child is likely to be born with serious mental or physical defects or abnormalities. This indication also appears in the new 1967 British law and in the recommended law of the American Legal Institute. Of course, a primary consideration here was to save the mother from the distress of bearing and having to raise a deficient child, but it was also considered that the life of a severely handicapped child was likely to be miserable and unhappy.

"8. *Abortion permitted unconditionally on the request of the woman.* The seven steps I have already described brought abortion law to the point where almost every condition that could be described as hardship for the pregnant woman or her unborn child had been covered. With all these conditions for abortion allowed, the logical question to ask was whether it was necessary to have a law regulating abortion at all. If in fact the woman could always find a reason that was legally acceptable, why not just let her decide for herself whether she wanted an abortion, and make it available to her if she did? Many people consider that this is the next obvious step to take in countries that have already taken most or all of the previous steps. This point has now been reached in several states in the U.S.A. But it had already been reached long ago in the Communist countries, in most cases without going through the previous stages at all. In the Soviet Union, after three years in which abortion had been totally illegal even on medical grounds, a very liberal law was passed in 1920. This was repealed from 1936 to 1955, and reintroduced from 1955 to the present time. I won't bother you with explanations of this complicated off-again, on-again policy. All that matters is that most of the Communist countries have now lived for many years with a state of affairs that allowed women to have abortions on request, without having to give any reasons.

"I think I have made it clear that the trend in abortion laws has moved overwhelmingly in recent years in the general direction of liberalization. But what we must understand is that we can't entirely judge what happens in a country by finding out what its abortion laws are like. Having an abortion is usually a very private matter, and it isn't at all easy to find out who's doing it and who isn't. The simple truth is that strict abortion laws have never worked. There are many women who are determined to have abortions, and if they can't have them legally they will have them illegally. Illegal abortionists have always found women ready to use their services and ready to pay them well. Occasionally the law catches them, usually when a woman dies or becomes seriously ill as a result of their operations. But no country has ever been able to stamp out illegal abortion—not even those in which legal abortion is available on request, because there are always women who think the illegal practitioner will be more likely to keep their secrets.

"People who study abortion laws have divided them into

76

three broad categories: restrictive, moderate, and permissive. Let's look at some examples of these.

"We have seen that all our traditional Western laws were restrictive, and some of them have remained so. Latin American countries almost all have very restrictive laws because they are nominally Catholic, yet in most of them abortion is very common. France still has a strict law, but it isn't taken seriously, and the estimate is that something like a million abortions are performed illegally every year. It's hard to make out a case for restrictive laws, because they don't really express what the people believe, and since they can't be implemented, the result is a tendency to undermine respect for laws in general.

"Moderate laws are best seen in operation in the Scandinavian countries. Many people think that Sweden, for example, has a very liberal abortion law. Some American women have gone there seeking abortions and have had an unpleasant surprise when they found it was not so. The grounds for abortion in Scandinavia provide for a number of options; but the point is that each case has to be carefully examined, and women whose reasons turn out to be frivolous tend to be turned down. Some of these turn to illegal abortion, which has not been stamped out. Some people in the Scandinavian countries would now favor a permissive law. But many feel that the present system works well, giving legal abortion only to those women who are faced with real hardship and stressing the principle that abortion is not a practice that any country should treat lightly.

"Until recently, permissive laws existed only in the Soviet Union, the Eastern European countries, and China. All has not gone smoothly under this system. The Communists hoped to end illegal abortion, but some of this still continues. And in some cases free abortion has been so widely used that the situation has threatened to get out of hand. In Hungary, for example, in 1964 the abortion rate went up to 140 for every hundred live births. The trouble was blamed on the fact that contraception was not readily available to Hungarian women, but attempts to put this right have not been very successful, and the government has been embarrassed by the whole situation. In Rumania, a permissive abortion law was passed in 1956. As the years passed, the rate of abortion went up and up, until in 1965 it had reached the incredible figure of over a million for a population of nineteen million, which works out at four abortions for every live birth. This catastrophic situation could not be tolerated, and the permissive abortion law was repealed. Bulgaria also, in 1967, gave up its permissive law, confining abortion on request to women over forty-five and setting conditions likely to discourage younger women.

"You may be wondering why I have not yet mentioned Japan. Many people think the Japanese have a very permissive abortion law. That is not so. The law might be described as moderate. Passed in 1948 and amended in 1949, it is called the Eugenic Protection Law. It provides abortion if the woman or her husband has a hereditary disease or defect or leprosy; if her health might be 'seriously affected' by continuing the pregnancy; or if she has been raped. What is permissive is not the law, but the way it is administered. The physician doesn't have to consult with anyone, and all the woman needs to do is to state verbally that she meets one of the legally required conditions. This is a good illustration of the fact that the *interpretation* of the law may be more important than the law itself. If the Japanese decided to take their law seriously and investigate all applications, the number of women who qualified would be drastically reduced. But as things are, the system offers the woman abortion on request. The peak point in Japan was reached in 1955, with reported abortions about 70 percent of the live births, but many abortions are not reported for various reasons (for instance, so that the doctor can cut down his income tax), and it is likely that in 1955 abortions were actually slightly more numerous than live births. Since that year the ratio has steadily gone down; even so, the total number of abortions in Japan, reported and unreported, is probably more than a million each year.

"In England also, a moderate law passed in 1967 has led to a somewhat permissive system. The law, called the British Abortion Act, allows abortion where pregnancy would be harmful to the woman's life, to her physical and mental health, to any of her existing children, and where there is 'substantial risk' of hereditary disease or defect. The law has been liberally interpreted by some physicians, leading to the setting up of 'abortion mills,' but the medical profession generally is far from happy about the demands made upon them, and there is general dissatisfaction with the fact that an estimated 10 percent of the women come from other countries where abortions are not so easy to obtain.

"Following this world roundup, let's take a look at the abortion laws here in the U.S.A.

"Almost every state, soon after it was admitted to the Union, passed a law making abortion illegal unless it was performed to save the life of the woman or to avoid a serious risk to her physical health. Some of the laws are rather vague in their wording, but what they were intended to do is quite clear.

"However, it has become more and more obvious in recent years that these laws have not been effective. As medical care of the pregnant woman has improved, the number of legal abortions performed has steadily decreased. At the same time, a vast illegal underworld has been performing abortions estimated to approach a million every year. The laws were clearly out of touch with modern medical knowledge and practice. For example, at the time when they were passed, abortion was a much greater hazard than childbirth. Today, this gap has probably been closed.

"In response to a growing demand for change, the American Law Institute included suggested revisions of abortion law in its Model Penal Code, completed in 1962 after a ten-year study. It proposed that abortion should be legal if the mother's physical or mental health is endangered by the pregnancy, if there is substantial risk of 'grave physical or mental defect' in the child, or if the pregnancy was caused by felonious intercourse.

"In 1967 Colorado amended its abortion law to include these indications. Other states followed, and by 1969 a total of ten states had done so, while California had adopted all but the ground of hereditary defect. In a number of other states, attempts to change the law were not successful.

"However, by 1970 a radically different approach was being widely adopted by the pro-abortion campaigners. Instead of trying to extend the laws by adding new reasons for abortion, action groups now began to challenge the constitutionality of all abortion laws, mainly on the ground that abortion was now safer than childbirth, so their original object in safeguarding the woman's health could now be better attained by repealing the law altogether. Another argument was that a woman's right to privacy included her right to decide whether she would bear a child she had conceived. In some states, as you know, the law has in fact now been repealed, and abortions can be had for the asking. At this moment the situation is very confused, and many legal verdicts are being awaited. There are some who think that abortion on request is just around the corner for the country as a whole. Others believe that the opponents of free abortion will mount a powerful counterattack, and the present trend will be halted or even partially reversed. I am not about to offer any prophecies about what will ultimately happen.

"What I will try to do in conclusion is to look at some of the arguments for and against a further liberalization of abortion laws, or their total elimination from the statute book.

"We cannot refuse to listen to the plea that women should not be condemned to accept undesirable and unwanted pregnancies. A great deal of hardship has been imposed on them in the past, and now that we have the means to end pregnancies with greatly reduced risks, we must consider seriously our responsibility to do so. This argument is fortified by our knowledge that legally refusing abortion to many of these women simply means that they will get it illegally. Although the horrors of backstreet surgery seem to have been greatly exaggerated for propaganda purposes, and it now appears that most illegal abortions have been competently performed by physicians; yet it is an injustice to women confronted by real hardship to compel them to go underground for this kind of medical service.

"We must also take seriously the threat of overpopulation that is casting a somber shadow on our world. When we look at the situation today in India and Pakistan and Latin America, and then look at the way in which a similar situation has been successfully avoided in Japan, we must recognize that, as a temporary measure at least, abortion can hold down the threat of excessive quantity of life that has the power to block all our aspirations to improve quality of life.

"On the other side of the balance sheet there are some troublesome questions. One concerns the legal rights of the unborn child. Almost the whole campaign for liberalized abortion has been concerned with the rights of the woman. This is natural enough because she is highly visible, can speak for herself, and has been doing so very loudly.

"However, just at the time when we have been accepting abortion and making it respectable, we have also greatly increased our knowledge about life before birth, and we are becoming aware that the unborn child is much more human at a surprisingly early stage in his development than we ever thought possible in the past. In legal circles there has been a trend to increase his rights as a person, or at least as a potential person. As long ago as 1795 a court recognized the right of an unborn child to inherit property and to be included among the children living at the time when the person who made the will died. Similar decisions have been made by other courts, including a case in which a female child was conceived on May 1, 1922, and was judged to be entitled to her share of the inheritance of her grandfather, who died on May 22, only three weeks later, and wished his estate to be divided among all his grand-children living at the time of his death. Children whose mothers had taken thalidomide, even as early as two or three weeks after conception, have also won cases in court for damages, and have been granted sums of money for their support. Damages have likewise been awarded to un-born children harmed by automobile accidents while in their mothers' wombs. Even when the child died in the womb from these injuries and never saw the light of day, he has been permitted to sue for damages. In 1969 an illegitimate child was even granted social security benefits on the earning record of her father, who was killed soon after she was conceived. The Court of Appeals ruled that 'Donna was viable from the instant of conception onward. . . . When the deceased wage earner came over for his week-end visits, he was in fact living with both child and mother.'*

"I'm not sure how we are to reconcile these legal trends toward recognizing the rights of the unborn child with the new abortion laws which allow the life of the same unborn child to be taken for reasons that sometimes add up to no more than the mother's social convenience.

"Finally, we must ask the question, What is all this doing to us? A very conservative estimate of the total number of abortions being performed in our world today comes up with a total of thirty million in every year. Even in our two world wars, casualties didn't come remotely near to this figure. Of course many will answer that there is a great difference between taking the life of the unborn and killing those who are visibly alive and mature. I recognize that this is true. All the same, you can't just say that it is of no consequence.

"At a world congress on family planning in Budapest a few years ago, great stress was placed on the need to under-take worldwide efforts to make contraceptives more easily available so that abortion could be avoided as far as pos-sible. There was considerable agreement with one speaker who said that abortion was inherently degrading. While most people today are prepared to accept it as a regrettable necessity, most of us also feel that a better way ought to be found of solving our problems, and we surely hope that it will not be too long before we find that better way."

* Details of these cases are given in Dr. and Mrs. J. C. Willke, *Handbook on Abortion* (Cincinnati: Hiltz Publishing Co., 1971), pp. 96-99.

"Dr. Kolb, I think you will realize that you have raised some profound questions for us and have left us uncertain as to how to respond. We recognize the spirit of sincerity and honest facing of the issues in which you have shared your great knowledge and also your unanswered questions with us.

"I had scheduled a brief time for questions; but we are running late, and from signals I have picked up from the back of the room I understand that lunch is now ready.

"Let me thank you once again, Dr. Kolb. You have more than fulfilled our highest expectations. We are proud to have a man of your caliber in our community."

Helen and I have arranged to take our lunch together in a quiet corner of a local restaurant, where we can discuss together what we have learned in the course of the morning.

Second Conversation with Helen

"Helen, I'm very eager to hear your impressions of this morning's conference sessions."

Helen gets out her notebook and flips over the pages in silence. Then she closes the notebook and lays it down.

"I think I should start with general impressions. On the whole, I thought the sessions were very good. The speakers really knew what they were talking about, and what they said was awfully interesting. Nearly all of it was completely new to me, of course. It made me realize how terribly ignorant I've been. I must also admit it makes my situation more complicated."

"Why is that?"

"Because I now have to take into account in making my decision a whole lot of things I didn't know before—or things I had all wrong. Perhaps I'd better be specific. Dr. Archer's talk quite upset me."

"I guessed that. And I think I can guess why."

"You probably can. I suppose the truth is that I really didn't want to know the facts about abortion. I just wanted some kind doctor to put me to sleep, get on with the job, and wake me up when it was all over. Then I would try to walk away just as if nothing had happened."

"Do you then regret that you were confronted with the facts?"

"No, I don't. I wanted to behave like a child and have someone else take all the responsibility. But now I know that just wouldn't have worked. I think it might for some women, but I'd have felt ashamed of myself afterward. I've got to stand up and face life as it is and take responsibility for my actions. I'm not a child, and I'm not an animal. I'm an intelligent human being, and this is a critical decision that could affect my whole future. I have to make it with the facts before me, just as I would make any other important decision."

"What were the facts that disturbed you?"

"The big one was that a decision to seek abortion is a decision to take life—only a beginning human life, it's true —and mind you, I think this could be justified for good enough reasons. But I've got to be very sure that my reasons are good enough. What Dr. Archer did was to show me how serious a decision this is. The friends with whom I have talked have made it seem a very trivial matter. I knew they were wrong, and I think they knew they were wrong. It was a kind of game to treat the whole thing superficially so as to avoid the real anguish that is involved. It wouldn't work—I'd only go through the anguish afterward anyway. I'd rather do that now and make a fully responsible decision. Then, if I choose abortion, I can go into the future with no fear that the thing will haunt me later and give me bad dreams; or worse, that it will make me callous and hard-boiled."

"Are you suggesting that what you heard this morning has tipped the scales against abortion?"

"No, only that it made it impossible to adopt a trivial attitude to abortion. Dr. Archer certainly did make it seem a hard thing to do. No, I'm putting that wrong. It wasn't Dr. Archer, it was the facts Dr. Archer presented that did it. But I was also impressed by what Dr. Ferguson said about the many people who are involved in an abortion decision and how the rights of one of them can never settle the issue. The conference gave me an awareness of my own rights and of my duty to make a decision that will be best for my future as well as for the future of others concerned. In other words, I saw that it could be a bad decision to let this new life develop, if the result would be a lot of misery all round. You know, it's easy for a pregnant woman to get very martyred and fatalistic about her unborn child. You can say to yourself 'I got this life started, and it's my fault. So I must accept my fate and atone for my irresponsibility by putting its rights above all others.' This could in fact be wrong thinking. It could be a guilty feeling that I am obliged to make it good for the new life, even if the result is to mess up the lives of other people, including my own."

"So the conference has challenged you to take a fully responsible attitude to the decision you have to make and to accept the need for really thinking it all out and for making a decision you can justify to yourself and to the other significant people in your life."

"That's right. And this helps me a lot. It gives me back some of my lost self-respect. A situation like this really gets you down. It makes you feel so rejected, so shut out, so wicked and inhuman, that you believe everyone would despise you and look down on you if they knew you were seriously considering doing away with your unborn child.

So you grovel and avoid people and wish you could sink out of sight. That's what I've been feeling up to now—this came out very clearly as I did the assignment on my feelings. I realized I was overwhelmed by a sense of my own inadequacy and inferiority, because I found myself in a situation where I couldn't do anything that would seem to be right and good. In other words, it would be bad to have the baby and bad to do away with the baby.

"But this morning, as I listened to the speakers, I began to realize that I'm not a stupid woman who is confused and perplexed while everyone else is confident and clearheaded. The tidy little packages in which official people wrap up the abortion problem are not answers to the problem, but convenient solutions they arrive at by looking only at one aspect of the problem and ignoring the others. The truth is that everybody who looks at this problem open-mindedly is as confused and perplexed as I am. I learned this morning that people have been struggling with this abortion question for thousands of years, and they are still deeply divided about the right answers. Each of the three speakers—learned men who had studied this for years—admitted there were questions he couldn't answer.

"Somehow this comforts me. It makes me feel I'm a member of the human race again. Of course these other people are trying to find answers from a theoretical point of view, while I'm deeply involved personally. They are looking at the problem from the outside. I've got the problem right here, inside. That makes a big difference. But it doesn't make all the difference.

"What I feel now is that I no longer want to lie down and die. I want to get up and face this thing and find the answer that's right for me."

"These are good things. Hold on to them if you can.

Did anything else that was said this morning impress you particularly?"

"Well, yes. Maybe this is just another way of saying again what I've said already, but I feel I got the abortion problem into much better perspective. I see it now not just as an agonizing personal thing I have to struggle with all alone in my obscure little corner. I see it in the perspective of human history. And I see it as a worldwide problem. As Dr. Kolb described how different countries were trying to cope with it, I didn't get the feeling that some were doing it right and some were doing it wrong. No country really has licked the problem, although they're all trying hard to do so. In other words, there are no perfect solutions, and what suits one country doesn't necessarily suit another. I think this is true of different people as well. There's no right way or wrong way of dealing with a problem pregnancy. There are different answers for different people, depending on their own personal circumstances. That means there is an answer that is right for me, and my job is to know myself and the facts about myself well enough to find it. No one else can do that for me, though other people can help a lot as long as they aren't trying to impose their solutions on me, but genuinely helping me to find my own. You know, a very interesting idea just came into my head."

"What was that?"

"Well, it occurred to me that maybe, when all this has been settled one way or the other, I might offer my services to Cynthia Boyd and her committee. Maybe someone who has been through it all herself would have quite a good qualification for becoming an abortion counselor. That would certainly be a very positive way of turning an otherwise very distressing experience to good account."

89

"That's a very interesting idea, Helen, but it's something for the future. Meanwhile, you have a very vital decision to make during the next few days. Do you mind if I bring you back to that?"

"Of course, you're quite right. Did you see what I was doing? Trying to leapfrog over my unpleasant present situation into a rosy future when it will all be over. That's another thing I discovered about myself when I tried to analyze my feelings. I didn't want to do it, because they are mostly painful feelings. I wanted to escape from my feelings, and you were pushing me in the opposite direction."

"I know. That was a hard assignment I gave you. It takes some real determination to walk up to your fear and your anger and your guilt and say, 'I want to take a good look at you and find out what you're trying to do to me.' It's much easier to run away and find some kind of entertainment to take your mind off your troubles. But then in the end you have to come back to yourself, and your fear and anger and guilt are still there. It's really better to face them, isn't it?"

"Yes, I'm sure it is. But most of us can't pluck up the courage to face them alone."

The Abortion Conference, Session 4— "The Value of Unborn Life: A Dialogue"

"It's time to get back to work. We have another full program this afternoon, and our speakers are ready to start. This morning we tried to give you some basic facts about abortion from the medical, social, and legal points of view. I think our speakers served us very well and gave us a good, clear picture of this very complicated human problem.

"This afternoon, we shall begin with the fundamental moral question that all our discussions of abortion keep coming back to—What is the value of unborn life? Instead of one speaker, we have invited two, representing very different approaches. Monsignor Kenneth Overton is a professor of Catholic moral theology who is on the faculty of the Holy Name Seminary in Silaston. Dr. Alice Thompson is Dean of Women at Westford College, and is known among us as a champion of women's rights. I'm going to give them about ten minutes each for short opening statements and then let them reply to each other. If there's any time left after that, we'll open the session for your questions.

"Monsignor Overton, we would like you to make your statement first. We welcome you to our community."

"Thank you, Mrs. Boyd, for inviting me to take part in this very interesting discussion. As you know, I am a Catholic and you know that we Catholics take a very clear stand on the subject of abortion. We regard it as a very grave offense against the sanctity of human life and therefore against the divine law. We have never really wavered about this, although in ancient times, when very little was known about life before birth, some Catholics thought the destruction of the embryo was less serious than the destruction of the fetus because in the early stage of prenatal growth the new being had not yet received a human soul. But in the light of modern medical knowledge we have abandoned all such distinctions. We now know that from the moment of conception a new and unique being exists with a life of its own and all the potentiality of growth into a fully developed person. Nothing will be added to this being from conception to the end of his human life, at perhaps seventy years of age, except oxygen to sustain his life and body-building chemicals to increase his size and develop the complex structures of his body that are already preplanned in the genetic package he receives when he is conceived. From zygote to embryo, from embryo to fetus, from fetus to infant, from infant to adult, all that happens is a continuous process of development. The various events that take place in his life don't in any way change his nature. The implantation of the zygote is simply the point at which he runs out of the original food supply the ovum provided and latches onto his mother's bloodstream. The birth of the baby is simply the point at which he switches his life support system from his mother's bloodstream to the resources of the

92

world outside the womb. His life is an unbroken, continuous process of development, not from the cradle to the grave, but from conception to the grave. All this is not the teaching of theology. It is the scientific teaching of biology.

"To destroy this life at any point is to kill a human being. If you decide that you are justified in doing this, you have crossed a very dangerous line. If you say, 'The embryo can be killed because he doesn't yet have a human identity, he doesn't have a name, and he can't speak for himself,' you can also say, "We can kill this old man because his mind is wandering, he doesn't know who he is, he has forgotten even his name.' You can also say, 'We can kill this woman because she has been so knocked about in an auto accident that she has lost the power of speech, and she can't take care of herself.' You can also say, 'We can kill this man because he has a long crime record; he is a danger to human society, and all our efforts to bring him to his senses have been quite futile.'

"In other words, once you allow the question of who may live and who must die to be decided by human judgment, you create a situation in which lives may be ended as a result of mistaken or biased opinions. Those in power can then decide arbitrarily who should be permitted to live— just as was done in Nazi Germany. You admit the possibility of a totalitarian state in which you can only be sure of your life if you are in favor with the party in power. You could even take us all back to ancient Rome where the father had the power of life and death over his own children, and no one could challenge this right. I don't say any of these things will inevitably happen in a country that approves abortion. What I do say is that in principle all these things could happen once you allow any mother, for her own convenience, to take the life of her unborn child.

"We Catholics therefore believe that we must take an uncompromising stand on this fundamental principle. It is the principle on which medicine has been founded from the beginning. To get medical help, you don't have to prove that you're an important enough person to deserve it. You don't have to prove that you have lived a good life or been a good citizen. Because you are a member of the human race, you have a right to live. There are no conditions, no strings attached. An unborn child is already a member of the human race. He already has certain legal rights. It is wrong and inhuman to put price tags on the unborn, to say, 'OK, this one may live,' and, 'Sorry, this one must die.'

"Once you surrender this principle of the right to human life, you are soon in trouble. You start with hard cases— the mother whose health might be affected by her pregnancy, the child who might turn out to be handicapped. But then people begin to extend the reasons. The mother is feeling depressed, so she gets a psychiatrist to say she might just possibly develop suicidal tendencies. She has a well-paid job, so the doctor agrees that her family would suffer too much if she had to give it up. Then you get down to trivialities, like the woman who wanted to terminate her pregnancy because she didn't want to miss the skiing season.

"Our Christian heritage is based on our profound respect for the value of human life. Our whole system of justice has as its cornerstone the principle that no one shall deliberately take the life of another, especially when that other is completely innocent, and the State provides full protection against any such danger. It is a sad state of affairs when this great nation with its noble ideals takes away that protection, allows and condones the wholesale slaughter of millions of the unborn, and debases the healing profession by requiring our doctors to act as public execution- ers and our nurses to dispose of the remains of their victims. This is not progress—it is regression to barbarism. I oppose it as a Catholic. But my opposition is not only based on religious grounds. The practice of abortion is equally an affront to all the humanitarian ideals of a civilized nation.

"Mrs. Boyd, that is my opening statement. Thank you."

"Monsignor, you have left us in no doubt about where you stand. We thank you, and you will have a further oppor- tunity later of taking part in the discussion.

"Now we shall listen with eager interest to our first wom- an speaker so far. Dr. Thompson, welcome to our con- ference."

"Mrs. Boyd, Monsignor Overton, and ladies, I appreciate deeply your invitation to me to share in this discussion. The subject of abortion is a very controversial one today, and we are all more or less exposed to the propaganda that is being poured out on both sides. What is unfortunate is that we seldom have a chance to hear these differences of opinion stated and discussed in an atmosphere of calm reason. I hope we are going to have an opportunity here to do just that.

"I do want to congratulate the Monsignor on the whole tone of his speech. I meet a lot of religious people who get fanatically emotional as soon as this subject is mentioned and who give you the impression that anyone who dares to disagree with them is going straight to hell. What I liked particularly was that the Monsignor based his case on hu- manitarian as well as on religious grounds. His argument was clear and forceful.

"However, my purpose in being here is to point out

95

that there are arguments on the other side, so I shall now try to present them. I'm afraid some of my women's lib sisters sometimes do this with a fervid emotionalism that matches that of their religious opponents. I assure you I don't intend to adopt that approach.

"I won't use this occasion to plead the cause of women's liberation. But let me just remind you that in the history of Western culture the woman has almost invariably been treated as a second-class citizen. I will concede that Christianity did a good deal to improve the status of womanhood, but always on the assumption that her status was subordinate to that of the man. Respect and even reverence were paid to her in her role as wife and mother, but let her try to act as a person in her own right and seek to share in the world's work and take part in affairs of state, and she was immediately slapped down. At long last, that era has come to an end and it is never, never going to return.

"Now that we women are taking a good look at the way men have treated us, we realize that our role in the past has been mainly that of objects of sexual pleasure and reproductive machines. We are not opposed to sex, but we will no longer tolerate any double standards. Whatever rights men claim, we claim too. We are not opposed to motherhood either; but since our bodies are so constructed that we carry the heavy end of the reproductive task, we insist on having the right to control how and when our bodies will be used in this way. And we insist on sweeping away all unilateral laws that stand in the way of this right.

"This brings me at last to the issue of abortion. I was quite impressed with many of the things that Monsignor Overton said. The whole idea of abortion produces in me, as a woman, a deep sense of repugnance. If I were ever in a position where I had to consider abortion, I would be very deeply disturbed about it. I wish women never had to resort to the termination of their pregnancies, and I look forward to the day when they won't need to do so. However, what I object to is the fact that our man-made laws deny this option to the woman with an unwanted pregnancy. Even if she never considered the option and never used it, she ought as a matter of principle to know that she could. To deny her this right is a violation of her freedom as a person. For this reason I am committed to fight for the repeal of all abortion laws.

"I recognize that the unborn child has rights. But so have other members of the human community, and the rights of one must be weighed against the rights of others. Of course we must respect the value of individual life. But has Christian society always acted on this high principle? Millions of men and women have been slaughtered during this enlightened century in wars between Christian nations—wars in which the fighters on both sides have had the blessing of the Church. It seems to me inconsistent for a Catholic chaplain to say mass for airmen who are about to set off on a mission on which they may bomb helpless women and children and for that same Church to disapprove of a doctor who aborts a woman to save her life. I am not trying to score debating points but only to point out the maddening complexity of human life in which we try to lay down absolute principles, and then find they can't be made to work. Just as the Church has had to make exceptions to the commandment, 'Thou shalt not kill,' in time of war, so exceptions should be permitted to women in times of crisis in their individual lives.

"I would not for a moment defend the woman who seeks an abortion for frivolous reasons. As a supporter of women's rights, I am not encouraging women to act irresponsibly, but the very opposite. I want them to have freedom in order that they may be able to take full responsibility for their actions, without being told by men what they may or may not do. I do, however, believe that situations may arise in which a woman *is* justified in seeking an abortion as the most responsible choice in a cruelly complex human situation. In other words, I hold the principle that unborn life may justifiably be sacrificed when this appears to be in the best interests of other lives that are involved in the total situation.

"Let me say one more thing, and then I think I'll have had equal time. We just can't be realistic in this kind of discussion if we ignore the threat of overpopulation that hangs over our world today. We seem to be rapidly approaching a point where quantity of life and quality of life can't coexist—one will have to give way to the other. And if we do reach the stage where we have to terminate individual human life in the best interests of corporate human life, it seems to me that this could be justified. We can already see this in action if we compare India or Pakistan, where all human progress is bogged down by the dead weight of excess population, with Japan, which is rapidly becoming one of the world's leading nations because by the use of abortion it has kept its population under control.

"My position, therefore, is that while I also value unborn life, I cannot put an absolute value on it. The rights of the unborn must be balanced against the best interests of the mother, the family, the community, and human society as a whole."

"Now, Monsignor, won't you respond to Dr. Thompson's statement?"

"Let me begin right away, Mrs. Boyd, by assuring you that you won't be called upon to intervene in a fight between Dr. Thompson and myself. We had a chance to get acquainted before the meeting started, and we immediately found that we could respect and like each other. I think I can speak on this point for both of us.

"However, I'd better make it clear to all of you that you have in Dr. Thompson and myself two immovable objects. We aren't going to be converted to each other's point of view. She seems to be totally committed to the principle that every woman should have the right to abortion on request. I am totally committed to the principle that induced abortion is wrong and sinful. You're not going to find any common ground between those two positions.

"Having said that, let me take up a few points in Dr. Thompson's speech. First, this matter of saying mass for airmen. I can't believe that any American Air Force plane would be sent out deliberately and exclusively to bomb women and children. But I do recognize that in the process of meeting armed force with armed force, civilians do unavoidably get killed in the cross fire. However, we Catholics apply here the principle of the double effect—your action is judged by its primary intention, not by any incidental result. I mention this because we also apply it in a situation which may involve the termination of a pregnancy. If a woman's life is threatened by cancer of the uterus and she is pregnant at the time, the doctor is permitted to remove the uterus to save her life (this is his primary intention), despite the fact that the unborn child will die as an incidental, but not intended, result.

"I would also like to make a comment on Dr. Thompson's fight to repeal all abortion laws. It may interest you to know that a distinguished Catholic legal authority has said that under certain conditions he would accept repeal of abortion laws. This is Father Robert Drinan, of Boston, who has now been elected to the U.S. Senate. In commenting on the abortion controversy, he took the position that rather than see the United States pass very permissive abortion laws, he would prefer to see no abortion laws at all. His point was that it might be more moral for the State to stand outside the controversy altogether than for it legally to support abortion on demand. Not all Catholics would agree with Father Drinan, but at least it is a position that a Catholic could hold.

"For myself I see great danger in the abolition of all laws. That would mean that as a nation we turned our back on the whole question and said in effect that people could do what they like. Generally speaking, I don't think the State should interfere any more than it can help in matters of personal behavior. But when it comes to the deliberate taking of innocent human life, I just don't think a responsible nation can abdicate its responsibility.

"There's a question I would like to ask Mrs. Thompson about this. If I understood her aright, she wants to campaign for the repeal of all abortion laws so that women may be free to have abortions on request. Then, this achieved, she hopes women can be encouraged to use their new freedom responsibly and not seek abortion for frivolous reasons. But it would seem to me that if women who take this view lead the campaign for free abortion, all kinds of other women, including many who don't take a serious and responsible view of the use of abortion, are likely to jump on the bandwagon. And once abortion is freely available, people are likely to become abortion-minded and simply take it for granted as the natural thing to do when you have a pregnancy that is in any way inconvenient. I understand this is what has happened in some other countries, with the same women coming back for as many as twenty abortions. . . ."

Dr. Thompson, who by this time is sitting on the edge of her chair, breaks in.

"Let me answer that. What you are implying, I think, is that women generally should first be educated and trained in the responsible use of freedom, then given freedom as a reward for their good behavior. If I may say so, Monsignor, you are speaking very much like a man. That is exactly the policy men have been adopting toward women for most of the world's history. Look at the question of higher education for women. For centuries men said, 'Women are stupid and can't benefit from education. So don't let's waste it on them.' Then, when as a result of not being educated, women sometimes acted foolishly, the men would look knowingly at each other and say, 'See what I mean? They really *are* stupid.' What you are now saying is 'Women are irresponsible, so don't risk giving them freedom.' My reply is that they can only develop responsibility by being able to try out freedom. They'll make mistakes at first, of course. But give them time, and they'll learn.

"There's a rather fundamental question behind all this that must be brought out into the open. The question is, 'Who in the long run is likely to care most about the value of unborn life? Men or women?' Men often talk as if the average woman would turn and murder her children at the drop of a hat if she were not restrained by a strong and steady masculine hand. But who lives closest to the unborn child? Who sustains him with her own lifeblood? Who carries him around in her body for nine long months, feels his first faint movements inside her, lives with him, closer than breathing, as a constant companion? Do men really think the average woman is ready to end the life of her unborn child as she would swat a fly on the window pane? If that's what men think, then it's high time they were properly introduced to women and got to know them as they really are."

Cynthia Boyd breaks in at this point and turns to Monsignor Overton.

"On the principle of equal time, Monsignor, I think I ought now to give you the floor."

"Thank you, Mrs. Boyd. Quite apart from her spirited defense of her sex, Dr. Thompson has also given us a pearl of wisdom. I like very much her idea that the children of the world, born and unborn, can safely be entrusted to the women of the world. Certainly it ought to be so. Maybe this is the great traditional concept of motherhood, with the sugary sentiment removed, making a comeback in a new, modern form—the demand for men to withdraw a little and let the women get together and restructure our society so that children really get the attention they deserve.

"Perhaps I, as a man, can ask another question. Obviously you're right in saying that no woman wants to murder her children. All right, tell me what we're doing wrong to drive so many women to do something that goes clear against their nature."

A young woman in the audience puts up her hand. Cynthia Boyd recognizes her. She rises to speak.

"It all comes down to the unwanted pregnancy and the unwanted child. That lies at the root of the whole abortion problem. Why should a woman find herself pregnant with a child she doesn't want? And what can we do to prevent such a thing?"

Cynthia Boyd turns to Dr. Thompson, who responds.

"Yes, I'll try to answer that. I agree with the questioner. Any woman who wants to get rid of her unborn child is in a state of desperation. She's acting against all her woman's instincts. So, what's wrong with the child that she doesn't want it? Our subject in this session is the value of unborn life. Why has this particular child lost its value in the eyes of the mother?

"I can give you some of the answers. Often it's because the mother is young and unmarried. She got into a sex relationship with some boy who isn't going to marry her, so she sees no way of taking care of the child. Also, her parents and the religious people in the community are going to make life pretty grim for her if it gets to be known that she's pregnant. So the best way out seems to be an abortion secretly arranged, so that nobody knows about it. What can be done about that one? Maybe she shouldn't be playing around with a boy, but she can't be blamed entirely when the glories of illicit sex are being shouted at her from the housetops. Maybe we women could do something about that. Meantime, we could see that girls get proper sex education, an integral part of which should be to drum it into their sweet little heads that if they are going to put themselves in the way of getting pregnant, they must use contraceptives, which should be available to them. Monsignor, I know you won't approve of that, but this is the women taking over, and you'll have to hear me out. Despite all we do, a few of those girls will still get pregnant. All right, if we value the unborn child, let's take some of the public disgrace away from this, make it practicable for these girls to go through their pregnancies and then give their babies for adoption to people who will value them and love them.

"Then there are the married women who get pregnant by accident when having a child would be quite a disaster. Often it isn't the pregnancy that is the problem, but the fact that they don't see how they can raise the child after it's born. All right, let's make it entirely respectable for a married woman to say frankly that she can't raise this child, but that she'll gladly hand it over to some other woman who will. What's wrong with that? I'm told the Chinese often do it. Surely we women, if we all got together on it, could organize this. And meanwhile we could get going on a massive campaign to teach the use of contraception to all our married sisters so that these accidents were cut down to the irreducible minimum.

"There's another group, the women who are pregnant with children who may be defective or who are the result of rape or incest. That's a harder situation to tackle, and I really don't see any alternative to abortion for most of these. But I guess they are only a small minority of the whole group.

"Well, there you are, Monsignor. There's a plan to cut down abortions to a fraction of what they are now. It could be put into operation by the women in our society—if we were really liberated and got the chance to take over. I'm afraid we'd have to employ contraceptives pretty freely, but surely contraception isn't as bad as abortion in your scale of values. You have to give a little here and there, you know, to get what you want."

The ladies enjoy this and respond with laughter and applause. The Monsignor responds.

"You certainly have some very good ideas there of which I could heartily approve. Regarding some of your methods, I would not be able to make any very helpful remarks. But I think there is great truth in what you say about married women seriously considering the possibility of having a child they feel unable to provide for and making it available for adoption into a loving home. I'm sure you are all aware that since our abortion laws became more permissive the number of babies available for adoption has dropped off sharply. I wonder if women considering abortion are having this alternative possibility presented to them really seriously.

"I would like also to refer to something else you said. It's about the very difficult situation in which the child may be defective. Often a specialist in these matters can predict the mathematical chances that the child may suffer from some hereditary defect or some prenatal handicap. For instance, in the case of German measles contracted by the mother in the first three months of pregnancy, it is reliably estimated that there is only a one-in-three chance that the child would be defective at all. A mother might well consider taking a chance on these terms that the baby would be all right. Of course we Catholics, as I'm sure you know, would accept the risk anyway because we don't think a handicapped child who is the child of loving parents will necessarily have a miserable life. In fact, it hasn't by any means been the physically fit people who have made the greatest contributions to human welfare. History is full of instances to the contrary.

"If I may, I would like to say something else about the idea of the unwanted child. There are unfortunate parents who don't seem to love their children, and even parents who abuse them. People often talk as though a woman who feels negative about a pregnancy shouldn't have the child because later on she is likely to treat it badly. But is this necessarily so? Doctors have often told me that pregnant women generally are quite ambivalent about their condition, and indeed, that most women during pregnancy go through periods when they feel negative about it. But later on they feel quite differently, and when the child arrives, they respond to it warmly and positively. Is the unwanted pregnancy really a reliable indication that it should be terminated? Or will the wanted child necessarily be better tolerated later on? I remember reading about one study of I think four hundred children who had been cruelly beaten by their parents. A careful investigation revealed that no less than ninety percent of them had originally been planned and wanted children. The study was carried out over a four-and-a-half-year period by Dr. Edward Lenoski, Professor of Pediatrics at the University of Southern California."

Cynthia Boyd is now looking at her watch. "Ladies, I think our time is just about up. But before we close, does Dr. Thompson want to make a final comment?"

"Thank you, Mrs. Boyd. Yes, there's something important I've been wanting to say in response to a point the Monsignor raised in his opening statement. He argued that the unborn being is fully human from the beginning, and I think he made a good case for that. I'm not much interested in haggling over words, but I think in this situation we could distinguish between being a human being and being a *person*. So we would say the embryo, for instance, is certainly a human being, a member of the human race. But he isn't a person, though he has all that is necessary to become one. He has a biological identity, yes, and in that respect he is unique—no other human being is or ever will be exactly like him. But he doesn't yet have a personal identity. That only begins to come in infancy, when the child makes himself distinctive by the special, individual way in which he behaves.

"The Monsignor compared the unborn to people who lost some of their capacities later in life. I think he was justified in doing this. The doddering old man who has lost his memory and his sense of identity has in a way gone back to where he started. He is less of a person than he was. You might say his potential had dropped, or had been lost. He can still be esteemed and loved for what he was, for what we remember about him. But what he now is is less than what he was, just as what the embryo is, is less than what he may become. I think this is recognized by primitive people in the custom that expects old people, when their capacities have greatly diminished, to go out into the bush and die quietly so that the others may have enough food to survive.

"What I'm saying, really, is that it is a serious thing to take human life, even unborn human life. But it can be justified when it is done in the best interests of other human lives. It's not as serious to take it before it becomes personal as it is after that. In other words, the earlier you take it, the less serious it is.

"I would like to add that I have thoroughly enjoyed this session. I think it represents the kind of honest exchange that helps us all to see the issues in proper perspective. It has certainly given me some new ideas."

"Thank you, Dr. Thompson. Thank you, Monsignor Overton. We now have a ten-minute break. Then we assemble again for our final session."

The Abortion Conference, Session 5— "The Need for Abortion Counseling"

"We are about to begin our final session. It has been a full day, but I know, from many of your comments, that you have found it most interesting and helpful.

"We are now going to consider the subject of abortion counseling. Our speaker will be Dr. David Mace, who is a behavioral scientist on the faculty of our medical school. His special field is marriage counseling, but he is very much interested in the need for abortion counseling and has helped us in the planning of this conference. After he has spoken, I will introduce four panel members who will react to his presentation. Dr. Mace, we welcome you and look forward eagerly to what you have to say."

"Thank you, Cynthia. We have had some excellent speeches, and I only hope I can measure up to the high standard that has been set by those who have already addressed you.

"We are here today to face the implications of a profound change which has taken place in our attitude to abortion. A few years ago, we would not have considered it a subject for public discussion. It was something disreputable that went on secretly in the dark. We knew very little about it, and since it was an unsavory subject, we were not inclined to investigate it.

"Now all that has been changed. Abortion is hotly discussed everywhere. Prestigious national bodies, including medical associations and church assemblies, have passed resolutions in favor of liberalizing the abortion laws or even repealing them. Changes in the law have actually been made, some of them radical changes, in several states. As a result there is a new climate of public opinion. Abortions are being openly performed for other than medical reasons in many of our hospitals. Women desiring help in terminating pregnancy can now call on various referral services, including one operated by the clergy. On our college campuses student publications are giving pregnant coeds directions on where to go to get abortions and even raising funds to help cover their expenses. All reports suggest a rapid rise in the number of abortions now being performed.

"While all this activity has been going on, very little has been done to focus attention on the human dilemma of the woman who has to choose for or against abortion. As soon as she gives indications that she is pregnant and is embarrassed about it, someone is ready to recommend abortion and move her on to the assembly line. As she moves farther along, her wish to terminate the pregnancy is taken for granted. There is no time to be wasted, and she is encouraged to move quickly. Most of the so-called counseling services don't offer counseling at all in the usual sense of the word. They exist only, or mainly, to control the traffic, to get the woman as quickly as possible to a competent physician who can do the job at reasonable cost.

"Some of these women are quite satisfied with this. Abortion is what they want, and they have no doubts or misgivings about it. The path to the abortionist is much more direct and much less fraught with hazards than it was in earlier times. For the woman whose goal is clearly defined, this is a bonanza.

"But for many other women the goal is not clearly defined. I have counseled with some of these, and I know the experience they go through. They want to know that abortion is an available option, and therefore they make inquiries about it. But they are by no means convinced that abortion is what they want. They are in a state of great confusion—mental, emotional, and moral. Added to this there is the time pressure—the clock ticking loudly in their ears. And it must all be kept secret. Often they can't discuss it with their families, and only with a few intimate friends. Even when such discussion is possible, they are likely to be neither informed nor objective. Nobody involved has a clear knowledge of the facts in any true perspective. What most of them have heard has been propaganda of one form or another. And many of them are personally biased, seeking to impose whatever solution they themselves consider to be desirable. Is it any wonder that the woman, especially if she is young, simply moves in the direction in which she is most vigorously pushed without ever really making a decision of her own?

"What counseling services are in fact available to this woman? There are of course competent professional men and women in every community—psychiatrists, psychologists, social workers, pastoral counselors, marriage counselors. But she probably knows little about the availability of these people to meet her particular need. She may make tentative inquiries only to find she can't get an appointment for several weeks—such people are usually heavily booked up. She may in any case need several interviews at short notice, and that introduces greater complications. Also, there is often the problem of the cost—she may be scraping the bottom of the financial barrel to pay for the abortion if she decides to have it. Generally speaking, the usual professional counseling services seem to be pretty inaccessible to this woman.

"The logical conclusion to which this seems to lead is that the physician to whom the woman turns should also be her counselor. This has been the view adopted by many advocates of liberal abortion—that this is a private matter between a woman and her physician. But a few moments of reflection soon show the inadequacy of this concept. The matter has been referred to several times in this conference. Provided the abortion is sought or recommended on medical grounds, and the woman has no misgivings about the wisdom of it, the physician is certainly the right person to counsel her. But how many abortion situations today fall into that category? An insignificant minority. For the rest, the physician lacks the time and often the skill to do what is required. Ethical decisions faced by women in a state of great emotional tension lie outside the competence of the average physician; and even if he were equipped to handle such situations, the hours of counseling needed would interfere seriously with his medical practice.

"Let me dramatize the crisis the woman faces by giving you two illustrations, both witnessed by a nurse in a New York hospital. The first was a girl who was having difficulty in making up her mind about abortion and was quickly moved through the routine hospital procedures in a state of increasing bewilderment and shock. By the time she landed on the examining couch, she broke down completely and was convulsed with sobbing that shook her whole body. The doctor was understandably taken aback and also somewhat exasperated. He faced the girl rather brusquely and barked at her the question, 'Do you or don't you want an abortion?' In despair she nodded feebly, and the operation went ahead. When it was over, the nurse told me, she was in a pitiful condition. But the doctor had no time for her, and the nurse had no time either. In the other case the woman, equally disturbed, had taken a night plane to New York at the insistence of her boyfriend, arrived at the hospital in the morning, had been aborted and discharged in the afternoon. In the limousine back to the airport she became disoriented, saying she had committed a terrible crime and couldn't go back and face her parents. Inquiries indicated the hospital from which she had just come, and she was returned there and left in the emergency room, where no one knew quite what to do with her.

"These are extreme cases, of course. But they dramatize, if in exaggerated form, the kind of emotional crisis a woman can go through. Consider how these experiences could traumatize the women concerned in their later attitude to sex, to marriage, to motherhood. And consider how much better it would have been if these women could have had the help and guidance of a wise and sympathetic counselor who could have enabled them to arrive at their own carefully considered decisions.

"I hope I have established the fact that there is a great need here, a serious gap in our social and personal services. Now let us consider just what the need is, and how it could be met.

"For some years I have served on a national committee of

the American College of Obstetricians and Gynecologists, and one of the questions we have studied closely has been the management of abortion services. I proposed during this discussion that no physician should normally be willing to perform an abortion until he was satisfied that the woman concerned had received counseling (from himself or from some other responsible person) that met the following requirements:

1. She understands what abortion means and is sure that this is what she wants.
2. Her own judgment is not being unduly subverted either for or against abortion by coercion from her husband, her parents, or friends.
3. In making her decision, she has considered how it will be likely to affect her conscience and her value system.
4. She has thought through the possibility of accepting the pregnancy as an alternative to abortion.
5. She is knowledgeable about effective methods of contraception and their availability.

"The experienced physicians on the committee had no difficulty in accepting these as reasonable requirements, although they had some difficulty in knowing how in practice this could be done. They were agreed that few doctors would be able themselves to carry out such an assignment. Yet if this kind of service is not provided, legal abortion could end up having some uncomfortable similarities to the illegal traffic it is intended to replace. The experience of the women I have just described makes the point rather forcefully. Hospital conditions of course lead to safer operations, but the horrors of illegal abortions have been greatly exaggerated for propaganda purposes—most of them were performed by qualified physicians who had very compelling reasons to avoid doing a botched-up job and having a dying woman on their hands. Even the economic discrimination which was such an undesirable feature of illegal abortion is in danger of reappearing in the legal services.

"Let us therefore take a look at what good abortion counseling ought to provide and then see how this can best be made available.

"Setting up counseling for these women presents some unusual difficulties. One question is, What name are we going to give it? In discussing it here we can use the term abortion counseling, but this would never do in dealing with the public or advertising the service. The woman considering an abortion wants complete privacy. She would be unlikely to go to an office with a shingle that said 'Abortion Counselor'; that might reveal her secret to prying eyes. For the professional person, some other designation known to include abortion counseling is necessary. Some women, for example, will come to me ostensibly for marriage counseling and then tell me in the privacy of my office that they really want guidance on whether or not to seek an abortion.

"In practice the abortion counselor probably has little chance of being directly approached by the woman. She will invariably come by referral or because she has heard through the grapevine that the counselor is ready to deal with problems of unwanted pregnancy. Referrals are most likely to come through physicians, pastors, or social workers, who are often very glad to know of a competent counselor who is available to help these distressed women. And of course referrals will also come through women who have already been helped by the counselor.

"Another serious difficulty arises out of a fact which I have already mentioned—that abortion counseling is always urgent. My own experience suggests that one interview is hardly ever adequate. The woman is often so confused, so uncertain about how she will be received, so ignorant of even the basic facts about abortion, that it takes the first interview to gain her confidence and to give her effective orientation to what counseling has to offer her. This means, therefore, that one may have to schedule two or even three interviews in the space of a week or two, nearly always at short notice. I have myself found this so difficult that I have had to limit severely what I can do in this field. If two or three women wanted counseling at the same time, one's schedule would be shot to pieces. And yet if one kept time open for this kind of work, weeks might pass with no requests for help.

"The whole situation is so complicated that I have come to the conclusion that the best answer lies in the direction of carefully selecting and training a small team of women volunteers, and I think this is what you plan to explore as a result of this conference. I'll come back to this later; but first, I want to go into a little more detail about the nature of this particular form of counseling, which is not quite like any other that I know of.

"The most important requirement, I think, is that the counseling should be decidedly non-directive. Our task here is not to diagnose and prescribe. It is to make available to the woman whatever information she wants, to respect her need to arrive at her own decision, and to support and guide her in this process. It is this acceptance of her right to decide for herself that she vitally needs and that is so hard for her to find. Her friends and relatives, if she has consulted them, are all trying to tell her, often vehemently, what she should do. If she goes to an agency that provides information on abortion and tells them she isn't sure she really wants an abortion, they are not set up to cope with this kind of situation, and they soon lose interest in her. If on the other hand she goes to one of the Catholic-sponsored agencies like Birthright, they are only interested in heading her away from abortion and would be discouraging if she moved in that direction. So the counselor must be open-minded and without bias in all his dealings with the woman. His only objective is to help her to arrive at the best decision of which she is capable. How does he achieve that?

"First, he will encourage her to tell her story while he listens attentively and sympathetically. He will ask her a few questions to get the facts straight, because he needs to have a clear picture of her particular problem. There are quite a number of different abortion situations—I have divided them up into a total of seven, and I'll come back to that in a moment—the counselor needs to know just what confronts this particular woman.

"As soon as possible, the counselor will encourage the woman to give free expression to her feelings. These women are usually in a state of great emotional tension and distress and very much in need of cathartic release. But they have also had to exert great effort to suppress their emotions, which are consequently under tight control. Their outward demeanor may show only indifference or defiance. This is necessary partly because they have a secret to keep and must manage somehow not to reveal their feelings to others, and partly because they are trying to adopt a 'tough' attitude to their own inner fears, anxiety, and guilt. The woman should be helped to let down her guard in the counselor's presence and to let her real feelings flow out. This may on occasion involve floods of tears, but this will normally be healthy and bring relief.

"The counselor should then help the woman to examine

the feelings she has now been able to recognize and express. Four general emotional states occur frequently—fear, anger, guilt, and depression. Those are of course all closely interconnected. It is helpful for the woman to ask herself and try to answer, just what she is afraid of, angry and guilty about. This may be a painful experience, because it may mean facing attitudes to herself and others which she has been trying to evade. But with support from the counselor, she will find it helpful to bring these deeper attitudes out into the open and find out what she really wants, which may turn out to be something very different from what she had persuaded herself she ought to want. A great deal of self-deception takes place in these women, and until they have recognized it, they are in no state to make good decisions.

"When the counselor is satisfied that the woman is back in touch with her true feelings, he can help her to move toward decision-making. Before she is ready for this, however, she will certainly need to know the facts about abortion, and the counselor will, of course, be willing to answer her questions.

"The woman should now be ready for the process of decision-making, which must begin by considering the various options open to her. One of these, which she should consider seriously, is the possibility of going on with the pregnancy. Abortion has become so much the 'in' thing today that some women give little serious consideration to any other option. I recall one girl who was quite sure her parents wouldn't consider the idea of her having a child out of wedlock. To her amazement they proved very receptive to the idea, and the experience brought them all into a closer relationship to one another than they had ever had before. I can recall also a woman who had been raped in her teens, but decided to go on with the pregnancy and offer the child for adoption. Her mother supported her closely, and the experience of bearing the child actually healed for her the hurt which the rape had brought about.

"In deciding what to do about a problem pregnancy, therefore, it is wise to begin by making the options as broad as possible. Closing the doors to any thought of continuing the pregnancy may sow the seeds of later remorse. The possibility should be fully and carefully considered before it can justifiably be rejected.

"Exploring the options means following through logically, as far as possible, the predictable consequences of each available course of action. It is best for the woman to do this herself in response to such questions as, 'What do you think would happen if you did that?' and, 'After that, what would you do next?' and, 'How do you think you would feel in that situation?' In this process the counselor can offer a good deal of help out of his own experience, by quoting such instances as I have just given you, in which unexpected possibilities appeared where the door had seemed to be closed. But care should be taken not to use these illustrations as veiled forms of persuasion.

"The goal of all this counseling is to encourage and help the woman to take responsibility for her own life and act as a free, autonomous person in accordance with her own values. It is possible sometimes to recognize the point at which she frees herself from the external pressures on her life and takes over her own destiny.

"Now let me take a few minutes to go over with you what I call the seven situations. Anybody can divide up the various types of women who seek abortion in his own way. This happens to be my way of categorizing them.

1. The unmarried woman who is pregnant by a man she doesn't want to marry, or who is unwilling to marry her.

That is to say, it is not possible or not desirable for the two parents to provide a home for their child. Often the girl is young, but she may be an older woman—unmarried, divorced, or widowed. The options are to have the child and offer it for adoption, to have the child and keep it, or abortion.

2. The unmarried or recently married woman, pregnant by the man she plans to marry or to whom she is already married, but to one or both the pregnancy seems inappropriate, usually on the ground that they are not ready for parenthood because of educational, economic, vocational, or other circumstances. The options are to revise their judgment and keep the child, to have it but offer it for adoption, or abortion.

3. The married woman who already has completed her family as planned and unexpectedly finds herself pregnant again. A special case is that of the older woman whose children have grown up, and for her and/or her husband the idea of starting parenthood all over again is unacceptable. The options are to change their minds and keep the child, to have it and offer it for adoption, or abortion.

4. The married woman who is pregnant by a man other than her husband. The options depend on whether or not the husband knows the facts about the pregnancy and about the paternity of the child. Abortion without his knowledge could conceal both facts from him. Keeping the child and concealing paternity is another option. Telling him all the facts offers the options of keeping the child with his approval, or keeping the child but leaving him if he does not approve. Other options are to offer the child for adoption, or abortion with or without mutual agreement. Clearly, this is a complicated one.

5. The woman (normally married) wants the child, but the physician's judgment is that it may be injurious to her health to carry the pregnancy to term. Her options are to take the risk and continue the pregnancy, or abortion. Fortunately, this represents a rare situation today.

6. The woman wants the child, but is told by her doctor that it may, as a result of hereditary or congenital factors, be born defective. The options are to risk bearing a defective child, or abortion. In this case it is important, by seeking specialist consultation if necessary, to know as accurately as possible what the risk factor really is.

7. The woman, married or unmarried, who is pregnant as a result of felonious intercourse—rape or incest. The options are to bear the child, keeping it or offering it for adoption, or abortion.

"Well, there you are. I made it seven. But I shall not be at all surprised if immediately this session is over several people come up and draw my attention to other situations I have overlooked.

"Just setting out these possible situations seems to me to confirm my belief that these women need counseling help. The situations are sometimes madly complicated. It seems tragic that we make no real provision for giving these unhappy women guidance and support.

"There are two other aspects of abortion counseling that I will only mention in passing because my time is running out. One is the involvement of other people in the counseling—the parents of a young girl, the woman's husband or boyfriend. The other is the need that sometimes arises for follow-up counseling after abortion, when the woman becomes distressed because of what has happened. Much of the follow-up counseling becomes necessary, I believe, because the woman got no help at the time she made her decision.

"Now I come to the last thing I have to say to you. What can we do about it? Very briefly, let me outline a plan.

"In Britain some thirty years ago, we worked out a scheme to use lay volunteers as marriage counselors. They were very carefully selected and thoroughly trained. They then worked under professional supervision and with access to specialist consultants. The system worked so well that it has been put into operation widely throughout the world, though not in the United States.

"Perhaps the need for abortion counseling can be met in a similar way. Couldn't women's groups and organizations set up the necessary framework? From a group of available volunteers, a few could be selected and trained. The services of these could then be made available to physicians, to pastors, and others to counsel with women faced with abortion decisions. Most of them would probably be housewives, and they could do some of the counseling privately in their own homes or be available to go to a hospital or clinic. They might take turns at being available on call for a week to deal with emergency situations. They would not be paid for their services, but reasonable expenses should be covered. I believe such women could be of great service to us, and I believe it would bring them a sense of fulfillment to be able to help some of their sisters in distress.

"I present the idea to you as a challenge. Earlier this afternoon, Dr. Thompson suggested that the women of the world could be trusted to create better conditions for the children of the world, born and unborn, if men would really let them play a full and responsible role in making laws and providing services. Likewise I am saying to you, this delicate task of counseling with the woman who is troubled about a pregnancy and doesn't know what to do for the best is from every point of view a challenge to the women of the community. We men need to recognize our limitations. If ever there was a job that women could and should do for other women in meeting a problem which is uniquely a woman's problem, surely this is it.

"So let me close, as Dr. Ferguson did this morning, by saying that we men are right behind you ready to offer our help and support. But this time, you are in front. There can be no question about where the leadership belongs."

"Thank you very much, Dr. Mace. Your plan will be most carefully considered at a meeting of our steering committee. And now, I will ask the members of our panel to react to what you have said. First, Dr. Donald Foster, who practices obstetrics and gynecology in our community."

"Let me say first, Mrs. Boyd, that I think this conference was an excellent idea. We ob/gyn people are in the front line as we meet the greatly increased demand for abortion which the new trends have brought about. I would be in complete agreement with Dr. Mace in regard to the five points he has suggested for counseling the woman seeking abortion. But I would agree that we physicians just wouldn't have the time to do this. Already our regular work tends to fall behind as we try to cope with requests for abortion, and we are having to turn a lot of the abortion operations over to residents and even to interns. I doubt whether these relatively inexperienced young men would have the skill to handle such delicate matters as counseling the women concerned. Indeed, I have to say that these abortions are creating problems for all of us—the doctors, the residents, and the nurses. We certainly need all the help you can give us."

"Thank you, Dr. Foster. Let me now turn to Dr. Michael Fellini, a psychiatrist on our medical school faculty."

"Yes, these abortion requests do pose problems. Under the old law, as you know, a woman could have an abortion if she could prove that her mental health might be impaired if she continued with her pregnancy. She would raise this with her doctor, and he would refer her to a member of our department. Interviews with these women were often very difficult. Sometimes it would turn into a battle of wits. You knew you had the authority to approve or disapprove of the abortion, and the woman was pulling every trick she knew to convince you that if you didn't sign on the dotted line she would sink into a deep depression or go off and commit suicide. You naturally felt sorry for her, but you also resented this attempt to manipulate you. We hated the whole procedure and were greatly relieved when the new law got us off the hook.

"As a result of these experiences, I am deeply convinced that any arrangement that puts the woman in the situation of having to find favor in the doctor's eyes in order to get an abortion is highly damaging to the doctor-patient relationship. The woman should have the final right to decide whether of not she wants an abortion, and her business with the doctor should be simply to arrange the details. A very interesting study in England showed that a group of doctors became quite upset and angry in trying to deal with women asking for abortions; but when they changed their approach and said, 'Yes, you can have an abortion if you like, but now let's talk about whether this is what you really want,' the whole atmosphere changed dramatically, and the doctors now felt friendly and compassionate toward the women.*

"I'm sure Dr. Mace is right when he speaks of the need of these women to get in touch with their real feelings and to make their own decisions. It's my opinion that most of the women who suffer emotional disturbances following abortion turn out either to have been pushed into the decision by a husband or boyfriend against their better judgment or to have made the decision in a state of panic in violation of their conscience, and as a result suffer agonies of guilt afterward. Both of these situations could be avoided in most cases by the kind of counseling Dr. Mace has suggested. I'd be all for it."

"Thank you, Dr. Fellini. Our next panel member is Mrs. Ruth Carson, a social worker who does family counseling in one of our community agencies. Mrs. Carson."

"I'm glad Dr. Mace referred to social workers as people who do abortion counseling. At our agency, we do all the things he referred to. We used to have a lot of pregnant girls coming to us to make arrangments for having their babies, and we counseled with them and sometimes with their parents. But now that they go for abortions they don't often come to us to discuss it beforehand. We wish they did. We're ready to help them if they need our help.

"If I may, I'd like to ask Dr. Mace just how these volunteer counselors would be selected and trained. Surely this

* T. F. Main, M.D., "Presentation for Abortion." Paper presented to the Third International Congress on Psychosomatic Medicine, London, England, April 1, 1971.

is rather delicate work to turn over to housewives? Is there time for Dr. Mace to tell us a little more about this?"

"I'll try. The object of selection would obviously be to make sure that the prospective trainee is suited to what Mrs. Carson rightly calls delicate work. She must be compassionate. She must not be shocked or offended by sordid stories. She must not be judgmental. She must be comfortable about discussing sexual matters. She must be objective and not have a marked personal bias for or against abortion. She must be capable of keeping confidences. I could go on, but you can see the kind of qualities we'd be looking for. These qualities can be investigated in psychiatric interviews and by psychometric instruments, which we could set up here.

"Training would include three components. First, knowledge of the field could be gained by directed reading and teaching seminars. Second, counseling techniques could be taught through role-playing of typical situations and case discussions and by enabling trainees to sit in at live interviews conducted by skilled counselors. Third, competence could be steadily improved by individual and group supervision. We have plenty of models to work with in setting up this kind of training program, and we would of course hope to have the help of experienced people like the members of this panel."

"Thank you. Now let me turn to our last panel member—the Reverend Richard Connor, who is a chaplain on our university campus. Mr. Connor."

"I find that at these functions the pastor usually comes on at the beginning to give the invocation or at the end for the benediction. So I'm quite at ease in this role.

"I get involved in plenty of abortion counseling. But I must admit I haven't felt very satisfied with the way I've handled most of these situations. I've learned a lot of things in this session that I shall now try to put into practice. For example, it never occurred to me to schedule more than one session with a girl wanting advice about abortion. And I'm afraid I have often just taken the girl's request for abortion at its face value, and never thought of asking her to consider other options. Yet I realize now that most of these girls are uptight and very much on the defensive and that this may just be their way of holding down their deeper feelings.

"So I hope I'm going back to do a better job. And if I get out of my depth, I'm delighted to know that Mrs. Carson is ready and willing to take over."

"Thank you, Mr. Connor. We now come to the end of our abortion conference. I think it has been a very useful project. As I said before, we shall be considering next week what further steps, if any, we ought to take. We are grateful to all who have contributed to making this such a useful day. The conference is adjourned."

Third Conversation
with Helen

It is Saturday evening at 5:30. Helen and I are in my study at home. We have been talking about the details of Helen's personal situation, following her attempt to examine her feelings in some depth.

"Helen, we've had a long, concentrated day. Not too much for you, I hope. Does your wrist ache with all that notetaking? Are you feeling tired?"

"The answer to both questions is yes. But I don't mind. I do appreciate the chance we've had to talk further over my personal problem. Now I suppose you would like my reactions to the afternoon sessions?"

"Yes, if you don't mind."

"Let's start with the first session. I liked that although it was a very serious subject, especially for me. I almost feel like saying it was good fun."

"I know what you mean. It was about the most pleasant exercise in disagreement that I have ever witnessed."

"That's just it. The Monsignor didn't argue or shout or dangle us over the mouth of hell, but he made his point, for me very effectively. I accept his reasoning—abortion is taking human life, and there's no getting away from it. Dr. Archer got that through to me this morning, and the Monsignor clinched it. But Dr. Thompson balanced it out so neatly when she pointed out that the value of human life isn't fixed—it goes up and down like the stock market. And I liked also her idea that it can be a human life but not a person.

"Well, anyway, I've got this part of my decision-making quite clear now. I see it like this. I would feel justified in ending this beginning human life if the benefits to be gained by me and other people outweigh the value of adding another person to the world's population who would happen to be my child.

"I liked also what Dr. Thompson said about women having abortion available as an option, even if they don't use it, because otherwise their hands are tied by men's distrust of their capacity to act responsibly.

"Well, all this enables me to see my task quite clearly. I have this abortion option. I am free to use it if I like. But my integrity will suffer if I use it without reasons I can fully justify. And getting myself out of a tight spot isn't necessarily a good enough reason. I must be able to point to the positive good that can compensate for the taking of human life.

"Now that's hard to do. That's where I feel I don't know enough about decision-making. How do I draw up the balance sheet? And do you act as my accountant and tell me if I've totaled it all correctly?"

"Let me try to answer that. I certainly want to help you about the process of decision-making. I've been doing some homework on that. But I'm not so sure about the accountant role. I suspect you may, perhaps without realizing it, be trying to get me to take over."

"Yes I do realize it. That's what I am doing. Why not? You're a trustworthy person, better qualified than I."

"But not qualified to take over your life, or anyone else's, and make major decisions. No, Helen, that wouldn't do. I can see you objectively and help you to take the right steps, but I cannot act for you subjectively. That's your privilege —and your duty. If I made the decision, you could blame me for it later if you regretted it, or feel obligated to me if it worked out fine. Either way, you wouldn't be taking your own life in your own two hands."

"I guess you're right. OK, I need your help in decision-making. What do I do?"

"We'll come to that very soon. But could we continue first your reactions to the conference? Were there any other points you wanted to bring up?"

"I like very much what Dr. Thompson said about women being capable of taking their full share of responsibility for children, born and unborn, if this responsibility is squarely placed on their shoulders. In spite of what she said about dominant males, though, I think we women may be nearly as much at fault for not taking responsibility into our hands. For instance, in this matter of undesired pregnancy, the woman will often put the blame on the man. But really, in most cases she is every bit as much to blame. After all, a woman doesn't have to get pregnant against her will, unless she is forcibly raped. In all other cases, she has participated enough to have to accept responsibility. It's much more honest to say, 'I got myself pregnant,' than to say, 'He made me pregnant.'

"The point about responsibility for children just reinforces what Dr. Thompson was saying all along, of course, that I must be able to justify a decision for abortion if I'm to act as a real woman. In some situations, a real woman might have to say that she wasn't prepared to stoop to the level of an abortion to get herself out of trouble, and that she was going to face the world and have her baby. That's a real option, though it takes courage. That's what Bernadette Devlin did, and she deserves admiration for it."

"I liked the attitude they both took to the unwanted-child argument. This is the one we always hear—'How can I possibly bear this child if I feel resentment because it's there, growing inside me?' But they answered this very neatly by pointing out that to someone else it could be very much a wanted child. Bearing the child doesn't necessarily place on you the obligation to raise it. You can give it for adoption. That's another option many women aren't prepared to consider."

"You sound as if you're moving away from the idea of abortion."

"No, that isn't necessarily so. I'm just trying to be honest enough to look at all the options fairly and squarely. I did start with the abortion one, by confirming my view that it could be justified. So as I look back, that session was particularly helpful to me. It did make all the options real.

"Now let me react to your session. In a sense, you were talking about what we're doing, so I felt this time that I was on the inside track. I was not entirely ignorant, hearing something for the first time as at the other sessions. In a way, this makes it a little difficult to evaluate.

"I thought you were very convincing about how much women need this kind of counseling, and you showed how hard it is for them to get it. I realized how fortunate I was to tumble into this almost by accident. Your five points indicating what preabortion counseling should cover made sense to me—I could think of nothing to add. And your summary of the four kinds of emotional states into which we women fall in a crisis of this sort exactly reflected my own experience, as you know."

"Helen, you could put it the other way around. These four emotional categories were taken straight from our conversation on Thursday evening."

"Oh, I mustn't forget the seven situations. Honestly, when you said seven I just couldn't imagine what was coming. But out they all came, and every one clearly had a different problem from all the others."

"Yet there are close similarities which they all share. Their emotional reactions are pretty well the same, allowing for inevitable differences in distribution and intensity."

"Yes, I suppose so. I recognized particularly the toughness pose with which we cover up our inner state of near-collapse."

"It's something people do in many stressful situations. Someone once called it a skin of indifference."

"That's exactly what it is. I thought you also brought out the self-deception we practice on ourselves in an attempt to make our problem a little more tolerable. It serves its purpose, but of course it can be devastating when it comes to decision-making—like a plane making a landing in the fog with its radar out of kilter.

"Finally, your scheme for volunteer counselors. It seemed to me to be sound and workable. But did you notice how Mrs. Carson raised her professional hackles at once? I think you may run into some opposition in that direction. The idea that mere housewives could do such delicate work. Yet some housewives are highly intelligent and competent people, mature and with deep compassion. It seems to me that raising a family could develop a listening ear and an understanding heart at least as well as doing social work."

"Now, Helen, it's time we got down to our last item of

131

business. We must talk about decision-making because this is our last scheduled appointment and the time is running out on us.

"I told you I had done some homework on this. While I was working on the final preparation of my speech yesterday, I thought it might be helpful to you if I tried to dream up some guidelines for the perplexed woman faced with a decision about abortion. It covers many of the things we've already worked at. It does have the advantage, however, of putting the steps in a sort of logical order.

"I got it typed out, and here's a copy for you. Perhaps 'I should have given it to you in advance. But it was only done yesterday, and you would have had no chance to go through it. So why don't you read it quietly now. I'll go through it again too, and then we can discuss it together."

THE ABORTION DECISION —
SOME GUIDELINES FOR THE PERPLEXED WOMAN

For many pregnant women, deciding whether or not to seek an abortion can be an agonizing experience. These guidelines offer you some help in the decision-making process. Much the best thing to do is to get the help of a wise, experienced counselor. But that may be difficult for you or even impossible. In that event you'll have to make the decision yourself. You may find it helpful to follow the steps outlined here. You will need a pen or pencil, and a supply of writing paper.

STAGE 1—DEFINING YOUR PROBLEM

1. You think you are pregnant. But do you know for sure? If not, go to a doctor (preferably an obstetrician-gynecolo-

gist) and get a pregnancy test to settle the matter.

2. You know you are pregnant, and you think you have good reasons for wanting to terminate the pregnancy. What are these reasons? Write them out, being as completely honest as you can. Don't stop at this stage to examine your reasons closely. That will come later.

3. Since you are in doubt, there are presumably also reasons for which you hesitate to consider abortion. Write these out too, as clearly as you can.

STAGE 2—UNDERSTANDING YOUR SITUATION

Before you can make a responsible decision you have to be honest with yourself. When you're in a tight spot, it's easy to make excuses for yourself and other people. Try now to see your situation straight, as it really is. Write out what you find and go over it several times to make sure it really represents the truth. Here are some questions to help you:

1. How did you get into this situation? How far were you deceived or exploited by other people, and how far were you yourself to blame? Are you the victim of your own folly, of the irresponsible behavior of other people, or of circumstances over which you and others have had no control?

2. Have you been handling yourself in this crisis like a responsible adult or like a frightened child? Write down a list of the actions you have taken so far to cope with the situation and decide in each case whether you now feel proud or ashamed of what you did.

3. How free are you to make your own decision? Are other people in your life—parents, husband, boyfriend, other friends, pastor, doctor—trying to tell you what to do or what not to do? Are other people trying to impose on

you their attitudes to abortion? Make a list of all the other people who are involved and how far they are trying to influence your decision.

4. Are there any other aspects of the problem that you're having difficulty facing realistically? If so, write them down.

5. Is it your wish and your intention to make this decision freely and using your own best judgment, and to be ready to face its implications and to accept the consequences? If the answer is yes, write a statement to that effect. If the answer is no, write a statement explaining why.

STAGE 3—INTERPRETING YOUR FEELINGS

Making decisions is very much influenced by your emotional state. Most women considering abortion are under the influence of very strong emotions. Try now to bring these emotions into the open and understand what they are doing to you.

1. One of your emotions is sure to be *fear*. Do you feel anxious, disturbed, sometimes on the verge of panic? Take a good look at your fears. What exactly are you afraid of? Is it the judgment and rejection of others? Is it the physical and emotional consequences to yourself? Write down carefully everything you are afraid of and exactly why this is so.

2. Another emotion you probably have is *anger*. Do you find hostility and rage in yourself? Again, write down what you find. With whom are you angry? The man who made you pregnant? Yourself? Some of your relatives and friends? Society in general? Ask yourself just why you are angry in each case, and write it all down.

3. You may have feelings of *guilt and shame*. Do you feel you have done wrong, or would be doing wrong if you went ahead and had an abortion? Is your conscience trou-

bled about it? If so, ask yourself exactly why you feel that way, and write it down.

4. Another likely emotion is *depression*. Do you feel that a dark shadow hangs over your life and produces in you a mood of despair? Do you find it a great effort to face other people and feel you want to crawl away and hide? Has the idea of suicide passed through your mind, even remotely? Write down any depressed feelings you have and why you think you have them.

STAGE 4—KNOWING THE FACTS

Good decisions depend on two things—your feelings and the facts. Sensible action must be based on reliable information.

1. How clearly do you understand just what an abortion is, and what it would be likely to involve in your case? Do you know where you can have the operation performed, and how much it is likely to cost? Does your state law allow it locally, or would you have to travel elsewhere? If you don't have accurate information on these matters, you should take steps to get it without delay.

2. You must be aware that abortion is a very controversial question. How far do you understand the arguments on both sides? Try to write down the case against abortion, and the case for abortion, as you have heard them stated. Try to be equally fair to both sides.

3. How do you yourself see abortion as a moral issue? Which of the following statements most nearly represent your attitude? (1) Abortion is the murder of the innocent. (2) Abortion involves the taking of human life, but only *potential* human life, which isn't murder. (3) Abortion is justified when the alternative would be very harmful to

other people. The rights of the unborn must be weighed against the rights of others. (4) Abortion spares a child the fate of being unwanted, and can be justified on that ground. (5) Abortion is taking life; but there are too many people in the world anyway, so it's good not to add any more. (6) Abortion isn't a moral issue. It is simply the removal of part of the woman's body and equivalent to taking out her appendix. If none of the statements satisfies you, write out one of your own.

STAGE 5—EXAMINING YOUR OPTIONS

Abortion is never the only course of action open to a pregnant woman. So before you decide, you should look at the other possibilities as well and try to consider what they might involve. No option should be rejected out of hand— that usually means irrational prejudice. The importance of looking at the other options now is to avoid nagging doubts afterward that it might have been better if you had done something else. Try, therefore, in each case to consider what choosing each option might mean to you now, a year from now, and five years from now. As before, write down your findings. Here are your options:

1. You could accept the pregnancy, bear the child, and keep it, trying to be a good mother to it. Consider this carefully, then list the arguments in favor of this action and the arguments against it.

2. You could accept the pregnancy, bear the child, and offer it for adoption into a family where it could be loved and cared for. Again, list the arguments for and against.

3. You could have an abortion. Once more, list the arguments for and against.

Now go back over all these arguments, try to weigh the

issues, and then list the three options in the order that seems best for you. This represents a tentative decision. But you aren't finished yet.

STAGE 6—MAKING UP YOUR MIND

You should now have written out a rather full account of your feelings, attitudes, and views about the decision you have to make, and even have registered a tentative decision. Now put this statement away, forget about it if you can, and after two or three days go back over it and see if it still represents your position. Do this several times if necessary. Moods and feelings change, and it is important that you should end up with statements you still consider to be correct each time you come back to them.

When you have reached this stage, you have finished with the statements. Put them away. Once you have made your decision and acted on it, you may want to destroy what you have written down. But you might also want to put it in a sealed envelope and store it in a place where it will be safe from prying eyes. If ever in the future you should have doubts about what you did, you can go back to the tangible evidence that you didn't make your decision lightly, but honestly and sincerely tried to act in a really responsible manner.

The final decision shouldn't be made in terms of reason alone. That's why the written statements should now be put away. The heart too, as someone once said, has its reasons. A woman, particularly, learns to trust her intuitions. And so she should. There are voices deep within us to which we should listen; though not without also using our rational minds. So now take enough time to listen to those deep voices within you. Meditate on the decision you have made and see if you are comfortable with it. For a true decision, mind and heart must be brought into harmony. Once this has been achieved, you should have a decision you can live with; and in a matter of such critical importance as deciding the outcome of a pregnancy, nothing less than that should be acceptable.

Helen has been studying the document and making some pencil marks on it. She looks up with a wry smile.

"As the Quakers say, 'it speaks to my condition.' "

"Helen, a little earlier you tried to assign me a role as your accountant to check your balancing of the issues for you. I declined that role for reasons I think I made very clear. This is the alternative I offer you, which I think is a better one. It represents the best help I know how to give you at this point, as I leave you to make your own carefully considered and responsible choice for yourself. I can have no part or lot in the final process of making the decision. My role as your counselor would not permit me to do so."

"Dr. Mace, you are right. Do you remember, when I first came to see you, what was almost the first thing I said?"

"Yes, I do. I asked how you saw my role as counselor. You replied that you knew I couldn't make the decision for you, and that in fact you didn't want me to."

"Right. Of course you are aware that on one or two occasions I have gone back on that and tried to lean on you for support. This was a very natural thing to do because I had been feeling very much alone and very unsure of myself. But you have done something much better than taking over and solving my problem for me. You have given me back the self-respect and self-confidence I had lost so that I can now, to use your own words, take my destiny into my own two hands."

Epilogue

It doesn't really matter what Helen decided. She clearly understood her options, and she made her choice to the best of her ability. It was not my task as her counselor to influence her one way or the other—only to help her freely to decide for herself.

And now, you also have to decide. I cannot know what your decision will be. But it is my hope that as a result of reading this book, you now understand the issues more clearly, and that this will enable you also to "take your destiny into your own two hands" and to make a choice you can live with comfortably in the coming years.

Resources:

FURTHER READING MATERIALS

As indicated in the Preface, I wrote this book to fill a gap in the literature. A great deal of material has been written about abortion. Most of it falls into two categories. The first consists of technical material—articles in professional and scientific journals, many of them reporting the findings of study and research. The second category consists of books and articles addressed to the general public.

I doubt whether you are likely to be interested in the technical material. Most of it falls into the fields of medicine, law, biology, moral theology, and the behavioral sciences. It would be inappropriate, in a book of this kind, to try to make a list of resources covering so vast an area.

A good deal has also been written for the public—some books and a great many articles in newspapers and magazines. Most of this material, however, is either written as propaganda, defending one side in the controversy and attacking the other side; or it is simply sensational. It is extraordinarily difficult to find anything written for the public on this subject that is open-minded and objective.

What I have decided to do is to give you the titles of only five books. The first two represent the propaganda literature—one on each side of the argument. Here they are:

Lader, Lawrence. *Abortion*. Boston: Beacon Paperbacks, 1967, 212 pages. This book, though now somewhat out of date, was written by one of the leaders in the battle for liberalized abortion. It is very readable and based on careful investigation, although the selection of material and its interpretation are obviously designed to support the writer's point of view.

Willke, Dr. and Mrs. J. C. *Handbook on Abortion*. Cincinnati, Ohio: Hiltz Publishing Company, n.d., 141 pages. Although nothing in this paperback says so, and religious references are avoided, it states in general terms the Catholic position. Its object is clearly to pile up arguments against abortion, which it does quite effectively.

The remaining three books are more objective discussions of the subject.

The Terrible Choice: The Abortion Dilemma. New York: Bantam Books, 1968, 110 pages. Based on the proceedings of an International Conference on Abortion, which was sponsored by the Harvard Divinity School and the Joseph P. Kennedy, Jr. Foundation, this paperback claims to be "a thorough exploration of opinions and facts on every aspect of the most devastating moral question of our age." It reports the many points of view expressed by the authorities who took part in the conference. The name of the general editor is not disclosed, but there is a Foreword by Pearl Buck.

Abrahamson, Harry and Julia. *Who Shall Live?* New York: Hill and Wang, 1970, 144 pages. This paperback reports the findings of a Quaker Working Party involving eleven people, six of them physicians, who made a careful study of our increasing control over life and death. It covers many controversial questions—the control of fertility, genetic manipulation, organ transplants, euthanasia—as well as abortion. Although the group come out in favor of the woman's right to abortion, they do face realistically the arguments on the other side. This is therefore an open-minded discussion, set in a wide context, and reasonably free from any flavor of propaganda.

Callahan, Daniel. *Abortion: Law, Choice, and Morality*. New York: Macmillan, 1970, 524 pages. This is a big book, involving a lot of reading. Yet those willing to work through it will find it a mine of information. The author spent four years of research in preparation for writing the book, went through all the literature he could find, and traveled widely throughout the world to see how abortion works in many countries. He sets out the facts with full documentation so that the reader can consider all the arguments on both sides and make a responsible decision. For any serious student of the subject, this is probably the best book that is available.

ORGANIZATIONS

There are many organizations concerned about abortion. Some of them exist mainly to carry on the fight for or against abortion; others to refer women to competent and reasonably priced abortion services, or to offer them alternative solutions that will enable them to avoid abortion. Some of these are local groups, rather loosely organized. I will confine myself to organizations working at the national level.

Association for the Study of Abortion, Inc. Composed mainly of professional people, the aim of ASA is to have all abortion laws declared illegal and to make abortion as routinely available as any other medical service. It has published *Abortion in a Changing World,* a two-volume report, sponsored a film on abortion, and publishes a quarterly newsletter. It claims to be the most widely sought and quoted source of information on the subject. The address is 120 West 57th Street, New York, N. Y. 10019.

National Association for Repeal of Abortion Laws. This organization has broadly the same goals as ASA but is concerned primarily with organizing and promoting action to challenge our present legislation. The address is 250 West 57th Street, Room 2101, New York, N. Y. 10019.

National Right to Life Committee. As its name suggests, this is an organization opposed to abortion. It undertakes national coordination of those who share its viewpoint and produces leaflets, books, and other material—a packet is available for $5.00. The address is Box 9365, Washington, D. C. 20005.

Birthright. Mrs. Louise Summerhill, a Canadian, started this organization in 1968, with the slogan—"the right of every mother to give life, the right of every child to be born." Her book *The Story of Birthright* can be obtained for $3.00 from her at 21 Donegal Drive, Toronto 17, Canada. Birthright groups have sprung up in many cities, and can be located through the telephone directory. Their main function is to help women with problem pregnancies to consider solutions other than abortion.

National Clergy Consultation Service on Abortion. This

headquarters office keeps information about local Clergy Consultation Services throughout the country and can furnish local telephone numbers through which recorded messages list the names of ministers or rabbis available for counseling with women trying to decide what to do about problem pregnancies. Some of these counselors do a thorough job of helping the woman to reach her own decision. Others seem to assume that she wants an abortion and simply refer her to an available physician. The national headquarters address is 55 Washington Square South, New York, N. Y. 10012. Telephone calls are answered electronically 24 hours a day. The number is 212-477-0034.

In addition to these organizations, which are concerned exclusively with abortion, information and guidance can usually be obtained about abortion services from family planning and planned parenthood agencies, and from the departments of obstetrics and gynecology in hospitals and medical schools.